John Ogilvie

The Theology of Plato

Compared With the Principles of Oriental and Grecian Philosophers

John Ogilvie

The Theology of Plato
Compared With the Principles of Oriental and Grecian Philosophers

ISBN/EAN: 9783337003050

Printed in Europe, USA, Canada, Australia, Japan

Cover: Foto ©Thomas Meinert / pixelio.de

More available books at **www.hansebooks.com**

THE
THEOLOGY
OF
PLATO,

COMPARED WITH THE

PRINCIPLES

OF ORIENTAL AND GRECIAN

PHILOSOPHERS.

By JOHN OGILVIE, D.D. F.R.S.E.

Και πως, ει μη Φοιβος αν Ελλαδα φυσε Πλατωνα
Ψυχας ανθρωπων γραμμασιν εκεσατο;
Και γαρ τηδε γεγως Ασκληπιος εςιν Ιητηρ
Σωματος, ως Ψυχης αθανατοιο, ΠΛΑΤΩΝ.

Epigram. ap. Diogen. Laert. Plat. Lib. iii. p. 213.

LONDON:
PRINTED FOR J. DEIGHTON, HOLBORN.
MDCCXCIII.

INTRODUCTORY OBSERVATIONS,

AND GENERAL ARRANGEMENT

OF THE SUBJECT.

THE character of the great author, of whose theological principles it is here proposed to exhibit a summary, has been held up so uniformly by the classical writers of all nations to the admiration of mankind; that curiosity to be made acquainted with the cause of an effect so universal, is excited in many readers by his illustrious name; which has been but imperfectly gratified. This circumstance is particularly regretted by those who know, that on that unbounded field wherein the comprehensive mind of Plato has expatiated, many objects occur of magnitude to attract the attention of rational beings, and of importance to merit the closest investigation. Questions that " come home to the bosoms of men," are proposed and examined in the writings of Plato; theories that originate in the most refined ingenuity, and that indicate the deepest research, are by him explained and illustrated; difficulties that stagger the timid inquirer, and sometimes overpower his intellect, are in many cases successfully obviated; and, in the course of various and complicated disquisition, philosophical discernment is embellished by the elegance of attic composition, and by the resources of the richest and most copious imagination.

I propose to exemplify these observations in the present essay, by an examination of the Platonic doctrines on subjects that are at the same time the most intricate, and most difficult of solution; as these may fall to be considered in the various departments of theology. The theories of our author on these topics, as well as his mode of expression, and peculiarity of sentiment, will appear

pear in the best light by being compared with those of other ancient philosophers, and particularly of his immediate predecessors, on the same questions. I shall therefore lay before the reader the tenets of the latter, on the various points which the present subject will offer to be investigated; as this view of the matter, while it may afford diversified and useful information, will most effectually promote the ultimate purpose of the following remarks.

The theological doctrines of Plato, which make a figure by far the most conspicuous in his multifarious writings, relate principally either to God, in the characters of the creator, parent, and governor of his creatures;—to the Universe, and to Man, the inhabitant who is best known to us, as being his workmanship;—to Evil, as originating in causes that are consistent with the divine perfections and providence;—and, finally, to the pre-existent state of man, the immortality of the soul, and the nature of that reward or punishment of which it will finally participate.

participate. On points that rise out of these principal subjects, Plato maintains peculiar opinions, which it will be proper to illustrate in a summary of his Theology: and the detail will be closed most naturally, by an account of the powerful influence of his arguments on the lives and characters of illustrious men; particularly in the last scene of life; and by observations that arise from the subject.

ADVERTISEMENT.

THE following Essay was originally written with the view of finding a place in the Transactions of the Royal Society of Edinburgh. It is offered to the public with some confidence, as having been honoured with the approbation of that learned and most respectable body, who were pleased to transmit their thanks to the author for his communication, by one of their Secretaries. The gentleman, (who performed this office in terms the most polite and acceptable,) at the same time acquainted him, by order of the Society, that the subject of the work prevented them from complying with his request, as " they were obliged by their regulations to exclude all disquisitions of Theology from their records."

The author is encouraged to present this work to the public, as well by the approbation of so respectable a body, as by that of individuals, who are high in the public esteem; and he will venture to add, even by the nature of the subject: for although Theology be not the darling study of the present age, yet attention is seduced by so many splendid ornaments in the theories of Plato, that they can hardly fail of obtaining a courteous reception even among the lovers of the Belles Lettres. The principles of our great author attract regard amidst those of other illustrious ancients, as predominant features of a countenance that are pregnant with character and expression, a truth that is illustrated in the present Essay by comparison. For this is the philosopher of whom Quintilian pronounces, that rising above prosaic tameness to a certain divine and Homeric elocution, his mind seems rather to have caught the afflatus of the Delphic oracle, than to be animated merely by human genius. Hence it has happened, that his maxims and opinions transfused into the writings of succeeding Greek and Roman philosophers, are blended so naturally with their principles.

The

The following little work contains the doctrines of Plato on the principal questions of Theology, arranged with those of the most illustrious among his predecessors. It has therefore some claim to attention, as professedly exhibiting speculations on the great subjects of God and the Universe, which may be said to have originated in *human sagacity*; and as establishing the truth of certain essential doctrines, by the testimony of mankind in the purest ages. In the illustration of Platonic maxims and theories, an attempt is made to explain certain obscure dogmas, by collating passages from different dialogues of this author, by which means his true meaning is discovered and elucidated; principles that have been ascribed to him without ground, by the most eminent of ancient philosophers, are set aside; his tenets in some cases are shewn to be the same as those of some great names among his predecessors, from which they were judged to be opposite; and charges that would imply inconsistency are refuted, if not with adequate ability, at least with that impartiality and candour which the subject seems peculiarly to prescribe. In short, an epitome

epitome of ancient Theology is here presented to the public, in which it will easily be discovered, that the author uninfluenced by preceding theories of whatever kind, has been principally solicitous of adhering to truth.

THE CONTENTS.

SECTION I.

Doctrine of the Ancients, and particularly of Plato, concerning the Divine Nature, Perfections, and Providence. Page 1.

Universality of the religious principle, and belief of the divine existence and unity.—Tenets of the Zabeans,—of Zoroaster,—of the Magi,—of the Egyptians,—of the Grecian poets and philosophers on the nature and perfections of the Deity.—Platonic doctrine, in what respect preferable to that of Epicurus.—Various designations expressive of the unity of God.—Explicit declarations of our author on this subject.—Application of the term ΘΕΟΣ to the Supreme Mind.—Explanation of the celebrated distinction of ΕΝ και ΤΑ ΠΟΛΛΑ.—Platonic ideas.—Mistake of Diogenes Laertius corrected.—Summary

mary of the Platonic tenets respecting the nature and perfections of GOD.—Comparison of the conduct of ancient and modern philosophers.

SECTION II.

Cosmogony of the Ancients. Of the nature, character, and offices of the persons of the Platonic Triad, as being interested in the formation, and government of the universe. Page 28

Cause of the attention of ancient writers to cosmogony.—Principles of the Chaldeans, Phænicians, and Egyptians, concerning the birth and generation of the universe.—Successive views of the doctrine of Thales, Anaximenes, Orpheus, and Pythagoras, on this subject.—Perfect consonance of Plato's account to that of Moses on a general summary.—Of the *Triad*, as concerned in this work according to Plato.—An obscure passage respecting their different offices.—Peculiar appellation and office of the First Person in producing the world.—Employment of the Second Person, under the denomination of ΔΗΜΙΟΥΡΓΟΣ, or ΛΟΓΟΣ, in this work.—Proper meaning of the term ΛΟΓΟΣ, the WORD, as used by Plato.—Mistake of a modern writer corrected.—The term applied strictly and properly to the Second Person of the Triad.—Introduction to the account of the Anima Mundi, or
Third

Third Person, in an examination of our author's principles respecting the formation and materials of the universe.—Refutation of those who ascribe to Plato the belief of the eternity of matter.—Schemes of our author and of Anaximander the same on this subject. N.—Mistake of Aristotle, in which he is followed by Plutarch, ibid.—Plato's account of the chaos more rational and intelligible than that of other theorists.—Examination of the constituent parts of the ΥΛΗ, or first matter.—Order of creation by the intermixture of various elements.—The whole mass actuated by the Anima Mundi, which occupies the center of the globe.—Objection of Aristotle answered. N.—Plato's account of this person.—Various hypotheses of his followers.—Judgment of the whole.—Physical office of the Anima Mundi as the cause of generation.—Moral purposes which he is employed in effecting.—Review of the whole theory, as applied to illustrate the obscure passage mentioned in the beginning. Its import fully ascertained. Concluding remark on the difference between the Platonic and Christian account of this subject.

SECTION III.

Middle order of beings. Inhabitants of the air and elements.   66

Causes

Causes of our belief in intermediate beings, who participate of the divine and human nature.—Doctrines of the ancients on the nature of demons or genii.—Points concerning these intelligences, in which they agree unanimously.—Opinions on the same subject wherein they differ.—Nature of the demoniacal body, being neither celestial nor corporeal.—Operation whereby it is rendered visible.—Division of genii into two classes.—Offices of the superior order—1. As mediators between God and man, in the opinion of the most illustrious ancients.—Judgment of Plutarch, Thales, Pythagoras, &c. to this purpose.—2. As superintending the rites of sacrifice, and as having dictated oracular responses.—3. As employed in chastising arrogance and criminality.—4. As beings who, for these reasons, are objects of worship and venetation.—Evil genii of this order.—Different opinions of Christian authors concerning them.—Nature and duties of demons of inferior order, their peculiar character and employment in the care of mankind.—1. Intelligences who have the charge of empires.—Genius of Carthage, of Rome, of Fortune, &c. considered as conducting great events and revolutions.—2. Genii of provinces, cities, &c.—3. Peculiar guardians of MAN.—Belief of mankind in the existence of guardian-spirits, and in their influence on conduct.—

Selection

Selection of these beings made, according to Plato, in a pre-existent state.—Guardians of Cain and Abel, and of Octavius and Antony.—Remarkable story of Plotinus.—Demon of Socrates sometimes mistaken.—Evil genii of this order.—Phenomenon of dreaming.—Examples of prophetical dreams.—A sentiment of Aristotle. N,—Genius of Brutus.—4. Dryads, hamadryads, satyrs, wood-nymphs, &c. genii of the last order.—Concluding remark on Grecian ingenuity.

SECTION IV.

Of the creation and constituent principles of MAN.
Page 93

Opinions of the ancients respecting the origin and constitution of man.—Pre-existent spirits.—Union of mind with body.—The latter purified by the former, and finally translated to superior regions.—Account of this matter by Anaxagoras similar to that of Thales.—His inadequate idea of the human soul censured by Aristotle.—Tenet of a sect of oriental philosophers on this subject, an improvement of the doctrine of Epicurus.—General remark.—Pythagorean hypothesis.—Explanation of the MONAD of Pythagoras.—Intellect distinguished by him from passion and appetite in the human frame, by residing peculiarly
in

in the head, and by regulating the latter which occupy the heart.—Use of the veins, arteries, nerves, &c. in retaining the divine and immortal inhabitant.—Man consists, according to Plato, of three parts.—Causes in the nature of man, wherein this distinction is founded.—Rational and sensitive soul.—Nature, office, and character of the former.—Sensitive soul how compounded.—Causes of its superiority to mere animal nature, to which it is most nearly allied. —Plato's remarkable account of the creation of man, as well as of the inhabitants of planetary worlds by the TO EN.—His separation of the rational and sensitive soul.—An account of their various operations.—Coincidence of the Pythagorean and Platonic theories on this subject.— General illustration of the universe of Plato.

SECTION V.

Platonic doctrine of the origin of evil, and its effects, compared with those of oriental, and of Greek philosophers on this subject. Page 109.

An inquiry into the origin of evil naturally arises from a contemplation of the phenomena of the universe.—Causes that led to it at an early period.—The three principal schemes that were invented to solve this difficulty, are those of Zoroaster, Chrysippus, and Plato.—Good and

evil

evil principle of Zoroaster.—Generation, and offspring of Oromazes.—Descent, character, and actions of his great opponent Arimanius.—Good and evil blended in the universe as the consequence of their contest.—Office of the mediatory being Mithra, or Miseles.—General observations on this hypothesis, illustrated by a remark on the *Satan* of Milton.—Advantage of this scheme above that of Epicurus, who denies the superintendency of Providence.—Chaldean and Grecian notions of this subject, formed upon the scheme of Zoroaster.—Stoical account of it contained in five propositions.—Their agreement in the belief of one Supreme Intelligence.—Causes of denominating this being Fate, Destiny, &c.—Chrysippus definition of Fate.—Origin of the Parcæ, or daughters of Necessity.—3. God, as being the necessity of future events, is, according to their doctrine, the author of evil.—Distinction groundless by which Chrysippus would avoid this charge.—Good and evil essential principles in the estimation of Stoical philosophers, which subsist necessarily together.—Plutarch's admirable refutation of this affirmation.—Observation of the author. 5.—The world, according to this sect, is a corporeal frame, of which the parts are spontaneously compliant to the will of Jupiter.—Consequence of this dogma as an account of the origin of evil.—Enumeration of the

b   incon-

inconsistencies and absurdities of the Stoics.—Cause of this incongruity.—Method of reconciling passages on this subject in the writings of the ancients, that are apparently inconsistent.—Excellent reflection of an ancient philosopher.—Plato unjustly represented by Plutarch, as maintaining the doctrine of Zoroaster.—The charge stated.—Answered by an appeal to the writings of Plato.—His modest declaration on this subject.—Two general observations made by him, that evil operates within a limited sphere, and in that sphere that its existence is necessary.—The true Platonic doctrine of the nature and origin of evil, contained in four distinct propositions.—1. Evils that originate in human imperfection.—Peripatetic principle of negation.—Question suggested by this inquiry concerning the origin of moral evil.—2. Evils that arise from the innate propensities, and tendency of matter.—These tendencies originally repelled by the Creator. Retirement of the TO EN into the contemplation of himself.—Consequences of this retirement on the state of the world, in which evil began to make its appearance.—Explanation of this doctrine, and remarks on it.—3. Theory and origin of moral evil, according to our author in the union of matter and spirit.—Two questions arise from this detail.—The first respects the present unequal distribution of reward and punishment;
—the

—the 2d. the causes for which souls are sent into this world from the abodes of happiness.—General answer that the evils of this life will be compensated in the next.—A more particular reply in the celebrated doctrine of pre-existence.—Platonic apologues.—Story of Er, the Armenian.—His account of pre-existent spirits, as well as of souls that ascend from mortal bodies, in order to be judged.—Scenes that pass before the entrance of the soul into its present state.—Purpose of this narrative.—Illustration of the Pythagorean and Platonic dogma of remeniscence, and of our author's philosophical idea of equality.—General remarks on pre-existence, as affording an easy solution of many difficulties.—Man at present in a state of exile.—How far this is a scriptural doctrine.—Two passages of the Old and New Testament seem to favour it.—Examination of each.—Pre-existence clearly an apocryphal tenet, although not expressly revealed in scripture.—2d. Question concerning the causes for which spirits are sent into this world.—Answered by another beautiful narration or apologue.—Particular explanation of its meaning and purpose.—Objection answered.—Summary of the whole section.—Evil, in the idea of Plato and Pythagoras, an accident, and transitory alienation from order, which will finally be corrected.—What ought to be the present occupation of man.

SECTION VI.

Doctrine of the ancients on the nature and immortality of the soul. Summary of the Platonic reasoning on this subject, and of observations on future reward and punishment. Page 166.

Testimony of mankind in all ages in behalf of immortality.—The voice of nature most clearly heard in ignorant and unenlightened nations.—Advocates of immortality more numerous among ancient than modern philosophers.—The system of Polytheism founded in the belief of future existence.—Philosophy and poetry concur in establishing this truth.—Nature and state of the soul according to Thales.—Notion of the Egyptian philosophers, of Anaxagoras, of Aristotle, of Hesiod, of Homer, of Cicero, on this subject.—Plato, of all others, the most strenuous advocate of immortality.—His observations ranged under five heads.—1. The nature of the soul. 2. Its desires and capacities. 3. Its moral perfection, &c. 4. Its hope of immortality, and the present unequal and imperfect distribution. 5. Its pre-existence.—His answer to objections.—1. The soul immaterial.—Power of the soul.—Nature of those objects which it delights in contemplating.—Its resemblance to the Divine Being, as a pure spirit, and consequent immortality.—It lays aside the body and grosser appetites,

appetites, by which however its researches are often impeded.—A true philosopher ought to wish for death.—2. Argument for immortality from the desire and capacity of the soul.—This desire is strongest in the best and worthiest men.—Effect of meditation of the divine perfections.—The immense capacity of the soul, a proof that it cannot be annihilated.—Socrates sublime description.—Other proofs of its comprehension applied to this purpose.—3. The moral perfection of the soul indicated by its participation of the divine nature, and its aspiration after the knowledge of God.—4. Arguments drawn from the present situation of man in behalf of immortality, and from present unequal distribution.—5. Sum of the author's proof from pre-existence.—1st. Objection that what we denominate the soul is an harmony of corporeal members, that is dissolved at death.—2d. Objection, that granting it to be distinct from body, it expires in its last form, after having gone through many metempsychoses.—1st. Objection answered from the nature of the soul, which is not dependent on the body as harmony on the instrument, but at all times opposed to it,—by the application of the terms more or less excellent to harmony, whereas more or less spiritual cannot be applied to the soul,—because the mind, considered as a concord,
ought

ought to be destroyed by vicious propensities that would be opposite to its nature, as harmony by discordant sounds.—Finally, because in music the harmony arises from the instrument, whereas in man the soul commands the body.—Answer, to the 2d. objection, that as principles diametrically opposite cannot subsist in one subject, the soul or principle of life cannot admit death, which is opposite to it, and would be destructive of its existence.—State of the dead according to ancient philosophers.—Opinion of a follower of Zoroaster, of Epicharmus, of Apollonius, of Tyana, of Aristotle, of Cicero.—Doctrine of immortality applied as consolatory to the unhappy.—Three states mentioned by Plato, as prepared for the unbodied spirit.—His account of the mansion of the Gods,—of Hades, or the state of purification ;—opinion of the fathers on this head.—Of purification, as fitted to different orders of men.—Gulph of Tartarus, for whom prepared.—Purpose of the metempsychosis.—Objection answered.—Doctrine of immortality applied by Plato to the purposes of life.—Exhortation to his disciples.—Sum of his whole argument.—A general view of mankind, as having been animated in all ages by the hope of immortality.—Reasoning of Plato on this subject contains, in the judgment of all succeeding

ceeding writers, whatever the mind could suggest on it.—Cicero's eulogium of this great master.—Effect of the Platonic arguments in behalf of immortality in the last moments of Socrates,—of Cato,—of Cicero.—Concluding address.

ON THE
THEOLOGY
OF
PLATO.

SECTION I.

DOCTRINE OF THE ANCIENTS, AND PARTICULARLY OF PLATO, CONCERNING THE NATURE, PERFECTIONS, AND PROVIDENCE OF GOD.

NO truth will be more readily acknowledged, by him who examines the nature of man, than that the religious principle is above all others, characteristical of the species. This principle is coeval in its original with the human mind; of which, in the history of all nations, it forms

forms the strongest and most predominant features. Men have indeed differed widely from each other, and will most probably continue to differ, in their notions of the various and complex branches of Theology. But their general belief of its leading truths is powerfully indicated by their attempts to explain its inftitutions, and to solve the difficulties, of which investigation hath in all ages been productive.

We may consider the following proposition as a theological axiom; that the first great object whom this science presents before the mind, is the Author of Nature, as His character is written in the volume of the universe.

> Ante mare, & tellus, & quod tegit omnia cœlum,
> Unus erat toto Naturæ vultus in orbe,
> Quem dixere Chaos, &c.
> Hunc DEUS litem deremit.

Ovid, in the present instance, may be considered as deputed to speak the language of mankind: for professed *Atheists*, in the strict sense of that term; are so few, either among ancient or modern philosophers, that they ought to be viewed as the solar maculæ, which, although they be discernible on the field of a telescope; yet, neither diminish the heat, obstruct the influence,

ence, nor obscure the splendour of that glorious orb on which they are permitted to revolve.

1. It muſt indeed be acknowledged, that admiration of the fabrick of the universe, gave birth at the same time to religious sentiment, and to idolatrous worship, among a simple race of men, at an early period of society. Thus, among the Chaldean philosophers, who soon became proficients in the study of astronomy; the ſect of Zabeans are said to have worshipped the planetary orbs, of whose revolutions they were often astoniſhed spectators, from the summit of their native mountains*. Nothing however is more certain, than that Zoroaster taught his followers to distinguish the Creator and Father of Nature, from his productions. I ſhall have occasion afterwards to mention particular circumstances concerning the life and principles of this philosopher. At present it is proper to observe, that he is not only said to have taught that all things proceeded from one Spirit or Power of

---

* Vid. Diod. Sicul. Lib. iii. and Cicer. de Divinat. Lib. i. cap. 41. among many others, where the Chaldeans are mentioned as proficients in astronomy. The latter writer observes that their pretensions to astrological divination were ill founded; upon the authority of Eudoxus, a diſciple of Plato, ibid. lib. ii. c. 42.

animation*; but that his definition of this Spirit as preserved by Eusebius, is at the same time comprehensive, appropriate, and sublime. Zoroaster says he, the Magian, in his sacred book of Persian Antiquities, has the following words:

" God has the head, (or eye,) of an hawk. He is the first of Beings that are incorruptible. He is eternal, unbegotten, immaterial; to whom no object whatever has resemblance; the Fountain of rectitude, and disinterested equity; the best, the wisest, the most excellent; the Father of well constituted laws; and the self-instructed, and sole MAKER of all things †." I have selected this passage particularly from many others of the same import; because it contains a more com-

---

* The words of the original are Εισεν παντα Πυρος ενος εκγεγαωτα " All things originated in one fire;" which I follow Psellus in translating, spirit, or power of animation, Pselli Comment. ap. Oracul. Sybillin, Amstel. 1689 vol. ii. a fine.

† Ζωραστηρ δε Μαγος εν τη ιερα συναγωγη των Περσικων φησι κατα λεξιν. Ο δε Θεος εςι εχων κεφαλην ιερακος· Ουτος εςιν ο πρωτος, αφθαρτος, αιδιος, αγενητος, αμερης, ανομοιοτατος; ηνιοχος παντος καλου, αδωροδοκητος, αγαθων αγαθωτατος, φρονιμων φρονιμωτατος; εςι δε και Πατηρ ευνομιας και δικαιοσυνης, αυτοδιδακτος, &c. Euseb. Præpar. Evangel. Lib. i. cap. ult.

prehensive

prehensive description in few words, than I have met with in the writings of any ancient author, on the same subject.

The Persian Oromages, of whom an account will afterwards be given, is described in the same manner, as the offspring of the purest light; whose perfections, benevolence, truth, justice, wisdom, and care, transformed by oriental genius into inferior deities, whom He is said to have framed after his own image; that they might accomplish by disseminating those virtues, purposes the most beneficial to mankind *. The Persians therefore, who saw the Supreme Being in every thing around them; considered the universe as his temple, and worshipped Him in the open air, by prayer and oblation †.

2. After all that learned men have written, concerning the descent of the Egyptians from Ham, to whom they paid divine honours under the name of Jupiter Hammon ‡; their original deities were the sun and moon, to whom they

* Plutarch. de Isid. & Osirid. Oper. v. ii. p.
† Herod. Lib. i.
‡ See Dict. Crit. Ant. Basnage Rem. B. & Univ. Hist. v. i. p. 445.

B 3   gave

gave the designations of Osiris and Isis*. The hieroglyphical appendages, as they may be termed, of their divinity, are more expressive of his perfections than the most significant epithets, when their latent meaning is comprehended and explained. An hawk, whose penetrating eye discerns the object of his search on earth, while he soars in the middle regions of air; is an image of the discernment, or rather, of the instinctive perception of Deity †. A serpent orbicularly twisted with its tail in its mouth, is an emblem of his eternity. His wisdom and intelligence are figured by the same animal, with the head of a falcon ‡. Under the human form, a complexion dark, and deeply shaded, emblematically pourtrayed the difficulty of accounting for his operations; the sceptre which he extends, denotes his imperial prerogative; an egg proceeding from his mouth, is an image of the world which he framed; and the

---

* This was the common opinion. But by Osiris, some Egyptians understood the Nile, the imperial river which fertilizes while it adorns the land of Egypt; by Isis, the region was understood over which it spreads in its progress; by Typon, the ocean, into whose capacious bosom its waters are finally discharged. Plutarch. Oper. Edit. Francf. 1620. v. ii. p. 363.

† Sybil. Orac. ubi supon. & Euseb. Psap. Evan. L. iii. c. 10.

‡ Auct. sup. calat.

plume

plume on his forehead, waving with every breath of wind; of the ease, variety, and celerity of his motion *.

It was in this land of mysterious wisdom, renowned for its fertility, and frequented for the acquisition of knowledge; that the sages of antiquity sought and gained instruction: and in the explanation of hieroglyphical characters, those enlarged ideas of God and nature opened upon the minds of philosophers, which have rendered their writings in all ages objects of research, and admiration. An ancient historian, therefore, is supported by the clearest evidence in acknowledging, that the theological opinions of the Greeks originated in Egypt †.

3. Among the poets and philosophers of Greece, distinguished from the earliest ages as the "lights of the world;" the first cause is occupied in different works, and is mentioned by distinct appellations, according to the particular purpose of the author. The God of Orpheus in the abridgment of his *supposed* doctrines, which was written by Timotheus, and preserved by Suidas; is the *Creator* of the uni-

* Eufeb. ubi fup. & cap. 11.
† Σχεδον δε και Παντα τα ονοματα των θεων ιξ Αιγυπτον εληλυσι. Herodot. Euterpe.

verse in the proper sense of that term, who brought order out of confusion; and is the fountain of life, wisdom, and felicity.*. It must indeed be acknowledged, that the Being who presides over all things in the Iliad, is discriminated widely from Him whom Orpheus holds up to us, in his nature and operations. In the former work, we behold Him, sometimes invested in the majesty of sublime description, with the ensigns of omnipotence; and sometimes debased by passions, and even by appetites, which bring him down to the level of reptiles of the dust. Alternately dignified, and mean; just and capricious; reduced to threaten when he ought to command, and to hesitate when he should be unalterably determined; we recognize in his conduct the motives whereby our own actions are influenced; and we justify Plato, in excluding from his commonwealth, the author of an assemblage of jarring qualities, so unworthy the sovereign of the universe †. Of Hesiod, I need only to observe, that his first mover, the offspring of earth and love, who brought the turbid elements into order, is clearly distin-

* Suid. de Orph. p. 357. Procl. in Tim. Lib. ii, p. 117. I consider the names of deities, and offices of which those names are expressive, as having originated in the same region.

† De Repub. Lib. ii. p. 604, Edit. Fixis. Francof. 1602.

guished

guished by the poet from his workmanship, as an original and intelligent cause *; a light, wherein we have seen that he is also contemplated by Ovid, in his account of the formation of things †.

In an explanation of the theology of the Greek poets, it would be improper to omit that of their dramatic writers, whose descriptions of the Supreme Being, are in general consonant to our present ideas of his nature, as well as to the language of scripture.—The shade of the mighty Hercules, is introduced in the Philoctetes of Sophocles, as addressing to that hero the following exhortation: " When you, with the son of Achilles, from whom you cannot be separated, shall have taken Troy, which must fall by my arrows; when you proceed in laying waste every hostile region; cease not devoutly to supplicate the Gods: for all things are under the government of Jupiter, the father, as well as ruler of the world ‡." It is well known, that the doctrine of Sophocles, in the preceding passage, is also that of Euripides; who addresses the Su-

---

* Theog. ab. init.   † Metamorph. ubi sup.

‡ Τουτο δε εννοισιθ, οταν
Πορθητι γαιαν, ευσεβων τα προς θε ς.
Ω; τ'αλλα παντα δευτηρ ηγειται πατηρ
Ζευς· Sophoc. Philoctet. a fine.

preme

preme Being as the Father and Governor of the world, at the time when he represents FATE as the daughter of his will.

Although the authors of those various exhibitions conceived very differently of the nature of God, and of the causes of events; yet they do not, in the same manner as many philosophers, confound the Creator with his workmanship. They pay honour to the Lord of Nature, as exalted above all other intelligences; and consider his power as exerted, at all times, with its proper effect.

The theories of ancient Greek philosophers on the present subject, will fall under review in the following section, wherein we propose to examine the phenomenon and origin of the universe. In the mean time, after having contemplated the God of the Chaldeans, the Persians, the Egyptians, and of the Grecians, in the writings of their poets; let us now proceed to consider the Platonic doctrine on the nature and attributes of this Being; a doctrine which constitutes the foundation of diversified hypotheses.

In an estimate of the opinion of our great philosopher on these topics, it is not a matter of much consequence to inquire with Plutarch at present,

present, whether Anaximander or Plato was in the right; the former, when he taught that the first cause frames the universe, by giving motion to the parts of matter, which he found originally at rest; or the latter, who said that these parts were agitated and disordered, until the Omnific Word interposed, and introduced arrangement, and symmetry into the system*. It suffices at this time to observe, that according to either hypothesis, the Author of Nature is distinguished from his production, as a MIND that possesses intelligence, and is the parent of disposition.

A reader of Plato will find, that no truth is more uniformly maintained in his writings, than the immateriality of GOD, as a Spirit who existed antecedent to Body, wherewith he ought at no time to be confounded. Among many proofs of this truth that may be drawn from his works, I shall only mention two, (as I wish not to fatigue the reader with unnecessary quotations;) which appear to me to be decisive. The first is in the

---

* Platon. Tim. ap. Plutarch. de placit. Philos. Lib. i. c. 7. The reader will see in the succeeding section, wherein this subject is treated at length, that Plutarch, and his followers were mistaken in their judgment of those two great philosophers, who maintained the same principles in accounting for the formation of the universe. Sect. ii. p. 50.

dialogue

dialogue, entitled Epinomis, where he establishes as the foundation of his reasoning concerning the Divine perfections, and providence, this principle; that " MIND existed before matter was produced, than which it is, he says, nobler, and more divine *." The inference arising from this affirmation, is surely too obvious to require enlargement. The same doctrine is taught in his Timæus, wherein he makes a very remarkable distinction, between " that which existed eternally without generation, and that which is always producing, though it never exists †." By the former, which the understanding perceives *to be always the same*, he obviously points out, and discriminates from matter the original cause of all things: by the latter, he understands the substance, or materials of which the world is framed; subject to mutation, and generating forms that are transitory, and evanescent.

By establishing as his governing principle, a maxim so consonant to reason, and so worthy of the Deity; our philosopher clears his system at once of the lumber, and monstrous absurdities of the Epicurean hypothesis, encumbered with

* Oper. p. 1008.   † Id. p. 1046.

material

material Deities, and fortuitous coincidencies *. He reasons from a truth, that has been confirmed by the testimony of mankind in all ages; and lays as his foundation, one of the most distinguished doctrines of revealed religion.

To the immateriality, it is well known that Plato adds, as a fixed tenet which he at all times inculcates, the unity of God. This truth is enforced with an attention, and particularity in the volumes of this author, to which it does not appear to me, that his numerous commentators have done justice : and I shall not perhaps do an unacceptable office to the reader, by entering at some length into the subject.

Among many designations of the Maker, or first cause, in the dialogues of Plato, the three following are peculiarly remarkable, as being expressive either of his nature, his mode of existence, (as it may be termed;) or his supreme dominion over all things. In the first sense he is denominated the TO ON, and TO EN; the former, as the great Being, absorbing as it were, and comprehending all others in his essence †; the

* These Gods of Epicurus are ridiculed by succeeding philosophers, and particularly by Cicero De Natur. Deor. Lib. i. sect. 63 and 91, &c.
† Vid. int. al. Repub. Lib. vi. and vii. pass.

latter,

latter, as indicating the exclusion of equality, or competition*. Another appellation that has great significance when applied to the Deity, is the term ΕΣΤΙ † HE IS, or he exists: for our author justly observes, that the past and the future denote inferior beings, who had an original; but that the present is the only appropriated epithet to what is immutable, and eternal. The last, and most common designation of the divine kind, is ΘΕΟΣ, God; of which we shall see afterwards, that Plato makes use with great, and *marked* propriety.

That the charge of Pyrrhonism may not be brought against our great philosopher, in a matter so essential as the unity of God; I shall select some proofs of his belief of this truth, which carry conviction along with them, from many others that might be mentioned for this purpose.

---

* Our author, by conjoining the designation ΤΟ ΟΝ, and ΤΟ ΕΝ in one sentence, expresses his belief of the divine unity in such clear and significant terms, as cannot be misconceived. The words are remarkable. Το γαρ ΕΝ, ΤΟ ΟΝ αει εχει, και Το ΟΝ, Το ΕΝ. Parmen. These words do not admit of a literal translation. Their import is, that Unity is the essence of Deity.

† Timæus. The similarity of this term to the I AM of Moses, will be obferved by those readers who believe that Plato was indebted for many doctrines to the Jewish legislator.

" It

"It must, he says, be acknowledged, that the space which we denominate heaven and earth, hath received many and peculiar advantages from its Creator. Those participate of body, and are subjected to change; but HE remains the same amidst universal agitation. Let us not therefore say, he continues; neither that the world moves itself, or that *two Gods* conspire to turn its course in opposite directions; let us consider it as being governed by one divine cause, Ὁνα Αιτια; and let us behold life, and immortality, as proceeding from its great Artificer *." In this whole passage we must observe, that Plato useth the singular number, ſυμνησαντος, &c. in characterizing the Supreme Being, with the obvious intention of establishing his unity; and that in the last part of it, he excludes the operation of two causes in producing this effect, and ascribes it wholly to one divine original. To the same purpose he elsewhere observes, that " One Being exists in nature, who framed all things, and whom we denominate GOD †. This Mover, or Supreme Intelligence, he describes, not only as pervading all nature, but as containing within himself, the beginning, the middle, and the end ‡." Is it possible to use terms more ex-

* Polit. Oper. p. 536.   † De Repub. Lib. viii. p. 750.
‡ De Leg. l. iv. p. 831.

pressive

pressive of belief in the unity, ubiquity, and omniscience of God? He who contains in himself the beginning, the middle, and the end, cannot surely have an equal: for no man will say that two Beings can exist, of whose nature these terms are expressive, more seriously than he would assert, that the incommunicable perfections, omniscience, and ubiquity, can pertain to efficients whose natures are distinct, and independent.

But why methinks it is asked, does this author, who maintains so clearly the divine unity in the passages above mentioned, adopt the language of his countrymen in so many other parts of his writings, wherein he mentions the *Gods* as superintendants of human actions; and points out particularly the means by which they may be conciliated, or appeased? I might have recourse in answering this question, to the popular distinction of the exoteric, and esoteric doctrines of ancient, and particularly of Pythagorean philosophers: and in following out the subject, I might affirm, perhaps with truth, that when Plato mentions the ancient mythological Deities, he purposely adopts the language of the vulgar, whose received opinions he judged that it was useless, perhaps dangerous to combat: on the other hand, it might be said, that when he discourses

courses concerning God as the author of all things, he uses words of which his disciples comprehended all the energy, while the less informed orders of men heard them without offence, or apprehension. But without having recourse to this distinction, the reader will perceive, that the passage which I am going to quote, while it contains the judgment of this writer on the present subject, throws light upon many other points of disquisition in his dialogues.

In the well known treatise entitled Timæno, Plato informs us, after having given an ironical account of the generation of the ancient Gods, Saturn, Rhæa, Jupiter, Juno, &c. that by these he understands certain demons, or inferior deities, who sprung from one great creator, of whose address to them, when originally framed, I shall afterwards have occasion to examine the purport *. My present purpose is to observe, that the words, while they contain an affirmation of the unity of God, who assumes the designation of Δημιουργὸς και Πατηρ, " the Maker and Father," establish at the same time a distinction between this Being, and those of inferior order, which our author carries on in general throughout his dialogues. An attentive reader of Plato will

* Oper. p 1054.

observe, that the term ΘΕΟΣ in the singular number, is most commonly applied in his writings, either to the cause of all things, whose perfection excludes equality, or to the other persons of his Triad, whose nature and offices will afterwards be examined. By the ΘΕΟΙ, on the contrary, he understands certain inordinate Beings, whose power, however great, and apparently extended, is delegated, and circumscribed. Thus, the rabble of mythological Deities shrink from the eye of our divine philosopher; and the Gods of the Iliad are secondary operators in the disquisitions of Plato!

From the preceding observations on the nature, and incommunicable attributes of the Supreme mind; the reader will be enabled to form some idea of the fountain or source of being, who was worshipped by the members of the academy. God, in their estimation, was one, eternal, immaterial, immutable, omnipresent, omnipotent, omniscient; the first and the last in the language of scripture; and in that of Plato, he who contains within himself, the beginning, the middle, and the end of all things.

Having thus established the unity of God as a doctrine of the Platonic school, I am naturally led to examine a tenet of our author, as far as it is connected with his theological principles; which is maintained invariably throughout his writings. I mean to consider here, (as the learned reader has already perceived;) the celebrated distinction of Εν και τα Πολλα, "one God, and many subordinate natures, or intelligences." It is proper to observe in entering upon this subject, that Plato delivers it, not as an original notion of his own, the result of experience, and observation; but as a tradition derived from the ancients, who were, he says, better men than those who lived in his days; and being nearer to the Gods, were admitted into the knowledge of their councils *.

We cannot hesitate to acknowledge, that our author understands by the ΕΝ, the Father of the Universe properly so called, to whom we have seen, that this appellation is peculiarly appropriated. The difficulty in explaining this dogma lies, is in ascertaining the precise sense of the ΤΑ ΠΟΛΛΑ, a subject that was much agitated among the ancients.

We may set aside without investigation, the notion of some writers, who suppose the *Triad*

---

* Οι μεν παλαιοι κρειττονες ημων και εγγυτερω Θεων οικουντες ταυτην φημην παρεδοσαν ως ενος μεν και πολλων. Phileb.

of Plato to be meant by this phrase, because himself declares that he includes under the term what it naturally imports; not a few, but many Beings *. In order to discover the nature and properties of these intelligences, we must consider our author's peculiar opinion concerning ideas, as far as it relates to the present subject. Without entering into the metaphysic of the Parmenides, wherein this doctrine is explained at great length; the following observations will, it is hoped, exhibit its general acceptation.

1. God, the το παν who comprehends the universe, is the great archetype, or pattern, in whom the images, or representations of all objects, whether incorporeal or sensible, are said to have existed before the creation of the world. Thus time, when it was created, is said to have been Παραδειγμα τι αιωνιου φυσεως, an image of the eternal nature: and the world in the same manner, is contemplated with pleasure by the Being who framed it; because, in corresponding to the original exemplar, it exhibited a beautiful resemblance of himself †.

---

* Ουκουν απειρον αν το πληθος ουτο το Εν ον 'ειη; Εοικι τι, &c. Parmen. Oper. Plat. p. 1120.

† Ως δε κινηθε τι αυτο και ζων ενενοηςε των αιδιων θεων γεγονος αγαλμα ο γεννησας Πατηρ, ηγασθη τι, και ευφρανθεις ετι δε μαλλον ομοιον προς το παραδειγμα επενοησεν απεργασασθαι Tim. p. 1051.

2. The

2. The models above mentioned, having subsisted in the divine mind from eternity, are denominated with propriety, as opposed to material objects that are evanescent, and transitory; "self existent, indivisible, and eternally generated *."

3. Those objects of which our senses take cognisance, are according to Plato's own distinction, imitations that had an original, of an archetype eternal, immutable, and intelligent, who is not perceived by sense †. It is obvious from this passage, that the images or forms ‡, (as Cicero denominates them) which subsist as ideas in the divine mind, are wholly different from the transcripts that are subjected to our inspection. Hence the world was eternal, as having subsisted, or, in Plato's language, *existed* always in the thought of the το εν, the Being who framed it; whereas the Το Μιμημα, the imitation of this great original had a beginning, and is an object of sight.

* Αυθαποτατος, Αμερης, Αειγενης Tim,

† Δυο διελομεθα. εν μεν ως παραδειγματος ειδος, υποθετεν νοητον, και αει κατα ταυτα ον, μιμημα δε παραδειγματος· Δευτερον γενεσιν εχον και ορχτον. Tim.

‡ Cicero substitutes the word Forma, as of the same import as the term ιδεα, in the platonic acceptation: and in this sense the Latin phrase has peculiar significance. Oper. Lond. 1681. v. i. p. 171.

4. Of these previous observations, supported by the authority of our great philosopher, the consequence is, that by the ΕΝ και ΤΑΠΟΛΛΑ, he understands, that all things are *one* when contemplated in their archetype, and *many* when we consider their nature and properties. In the former case, they are parts of a complicated machine conceived in the mind of the architect, wherein they have a fixed purpose and arrangement; in the latter, they are modifications that are perceived by sense. Our author's doctrine, however, on the present subject is in this sense peculiar, that the original patterns of his ideas are, as we have already seen, self existent, intelligent, and eternal. It was by this view of the subject that Plutarch was influenced in declaring, that according to the doctrine of Plato, three constituent principles entered into the formation of the universe; God, (or mind,) Matter, and Idea *.

In

---

* Oper. v. ii. p. 878. Laertius admits only two of these principles, God and Matter, without mentioning the last. Lib. iii. p. 228. It is somewhat surprising, that of those authors, the latter particularly, who professedly details the dogmas of our author, should consider matter as having been in his (Plato's) estimation uncreated, notwithstanding the most explicit declarations of the contrary in different parts of his writings. It is indeed true, that God is admitted to be the operating cause. But Plato assigns to this

Being

In the world of our author, which teems in every part with animation, we have seen that the living images, such as he describes them, correspond to his τα πολλα, so as to afford sufficient illustration of the maxim above mentioned. The ΤΟ ΠΛΗΘΟΣ, or multitude whom he mentions, will be found in the inferior divinities and demons of a middle order, whose nature and offices will come afterwards to be considered.

It remains, in order to exhibit a full view of the present subject, that our author's notions of

Being no other office in this great work, in the judgment of his biographer, than that of bringing into order discordant and jarring atoms, from whose combination he framed the universe. His part, therefore, was no greater than is that of a skilful artificer, who makes the best use of his tools, and materials. Laert. Plat. Lib. iii. p 228. The reader must have perceived, that this account is wholly diff'rent from that of Plato himself, who not only says that spirit existed before matter, but that God created heaven and earth; a doctrine for which he is very improperly censured by Aristotle, as we shall see afterwards. Epinom. p. 1008. De Legib. l. x. p. 949. Tim p. 1054. Aristot. de Nat. Auscult. Lib. 8. p 409, Lutet. Paris. 1619. v. 1. Now if matter were preceded by spirit, which is nobler and more excellent; whence had matter its original? Not surely from itself, for it is mentioned as a rude and unfashioned substance. Spirit therefore which existed from eternity, framed the materials of which it fashioned the universe. And Laertius, instead of asserting that spirit and matter were the principles of all things, ought to have said, that God alone in Plato's estimation, was their original.

the

the moral perfections and government of the Deity, should be subjoined to the detail that has been given of his natural, and incommunicable attributes.

The declarations of our great philosopher on this branch of his theology, are animated, as well as explicit. And his expression, dictated by the heart, on points in which he is deeply interested, hath sometimes peculiar energy and significance. A few examples will illustrate and justify these observations.

Plato distinguishes God at all times from every inferior object of pursuit. " Knowledge and truth proceed indeed from him as their original." But these do not constitute the *chief good*, according to the false estimation of philosophers. This ultimate desideration of the wise and the virtuous, is to be found in God only; in God, who as the sun in the lower regions, is at the same time the fountain of light, and of happiness[*]. This Being, the author of knowledge and truth, the liberal source of whatever is beneficent[†]; actuated at no time by malevolence[‡], and impartial in the allotment of reward and punishment[§]; regards the prayers of his creatures with peculiar

[*] De Repub. l. vii. p. 687.   [†] Epir. 1006.
[‡] Thætet. p. 112.   [§] Id. p. 129.

complacency *, and regulates by his providence the least, as well as the greatest events †. To the question therefore, which of all the works of God exhibits the most perfect resemblance of himself? our author replies, a good man ‡. Finally, inattentive to oblations that are offered from ostentation, and to requests which proceed not from the heart; he looks with benignity upon the just, and can be pleased only by a good life §.

Our author, after having enlarged in many parts of his writings on the moral perfections of the Deity, contemplates him, as being rendered by their combination, the supreme and ultimate object of desire. In this divine pattern of all that is beautiful, or excellent, he represents the το καλον, and το αγαθον, the standard of rectitude and goodness as being ultimately placed.

---

* Id. ibid.   † De Legib. Lib. x. p. 956.

‡ Epinom. p. 1008. There is no doubt a remarkable consonancy of every part of this account, to various passages of scripture; although not, in my opinion, sufficiently strong to justify the supposition that the writers were mutually acquainted with each other. The most striking resemblance is in Plato's description of God, as being pleased with a good life rather than with sacrifice, as corresponding to the sentiments of David's sacrifice and offering, &c. and of Hoseah, thus doth the Lord require of thee, &c.

§ Conviv. p. 1199.

And

And he follows the mind in its progress from the contemplation of simple forms, to that of consummate excellence; by enumerating the steps that lead to the summit to which it finally ascends*. He exhorts therefore his disciples, in an animated stile of the most sublime devotion, " to fly from this evil world, by becoming assimilated to the divine mind in that wisdom, justice, and holiness, which constitute the perfections of his nature †."

From the observations that have been made on the subject of this section, illustrated by examples, the reader may form some idea of the Being whom philosophy offered to her earliest votaries as the object of adoration. He will perceive from the rough draught that has been placed before him, their various theories on the most important doctrines, and will be confirmed in believing, by subsequent remarks, and illustrations, that the first teachers of mankind ascended by the dim light that directed their path towards the Father of the Universe. They acknowledged his being, discerned his perfections, justified his arrangements, confided in his wisdom; and left to the philosophers of modern times, conducted by clearer light, and possessed of superior advan-

---

* Thætet. Oper. p. 106.   † Id. ibid.

tages, the task of discovering, in the contempt of theory, the abolition of creative energy, the rejection of religious principle, and the reproduction of ancient anarchy; the extension of cultivated thought, and the traces of enlightened understanding.

SECT.

SECTION II.

COSMOGONY OF THE ANCIENTS. OF THE NATUUE, CHARACTER, AND OFFICES OF THE PERSONS OF THE PLATONIC TRIAD, AS BEING INTERESTED IN THE FORMATION, AND GOVERNMENT OF THE UNIVERSE.

IN the first ages of society, when principles, of which the effects are now conspicuous in the establishment of order and subordination, began to operate on the mind; men were naturally, and indeed peculiarly solicitous to be made acquainted with their own origin, as well as with that of the universe; and the first philosophers advanced by a process perfectly easy and comprehensible, from admiration of effects of which their senses took cognisance, to the investigation of an adequate efficient. Hence it is, that the few fragments of the most remote antiquity which have reached the present times, consist principally of hypotheses that were framed to account for the origin, and to explain the phenomena of the universe. The theories of philosophers, who may be properly denominated self-taught on these subjects, will naturally introduce that of Plato, whose knowledge was more comprehensive: and the reader will receive entertainment,

tainment, if not beneficial information, from the various objects which a view of this subject will place successively before his mind.

The Chaldeans believed, that the great Author of Nature, who is himself one uncompounded essence, the source of whatever is excellent, produced originally seven worlds; and that our earth, the last in estimation and utility, was placed beneath the lunar orb. It was therefore denominated Μισηφανις, on account of its darkness and opacity. Of those they taught, that one was composed of pure fire, three of ethereal substance, and the others of a grosser matter, somewhat similar to that of our own mansion, which contained the συθηγ, the foundation, or rude materials, of nobler and more perfect workmanship. From productions composed of such discordant materials, they judged that suitable governors were appointed by the Supreme Being; the first and principal Ruler being composed of the element of fire, the second of ether, and the last of matter, accommodated to their various spheres of operation *. The learned reader will observe a similarity of this mundane doctrine of the Chaldeans, to the notions of Socrates in the celebrated dialogue entitled Phedon; which would induce a belief, that he had either approved of, and adopted

* Pselli Summer. Dogmat. Chaldaic. p. 110.

adopted some part of their principles, from conviction, that they were well founded; or that the coincidence had been occasioned by the spontaneous ideas which the subject excited in his mind *.

Whoever may consider the Phænician doctrine concerning the origin of the universe as it is detailed by Sanchaniatho; will find in it the rudiments of a scheme that was adopted by Hesiod, and was improved afterwards into a regular system, by the labour of succeeding philosophers †. The dark spirit, and the fluctuating chaos brought into order by voluntary and imperceptible motion that produced desire; while it brings to our minds the generation of heaven, from earth and love, in the language of the poet; exhibits a striking proof, that in the judgement of the first teachers of mankind, the purpose of the Deity, in fashioning the world, was the benevolent motive of producing arrangement. And it cannot

* Phed. ap. Plat. Dial. Oxon. 1752. p. 289, &c. It ought particularly to be observed, that Socrates considers in the same manner as our Chaldean philosophers this earth, as consisting of dregs, or sediment, when compared with the etherial regions, and the worlds on which he directs that their attention should be fixed. Αυτην δε την γην καθαραν εν καθαρω κεισθαι τω ερανω—ε δε υποσταθμην ταυτα ειναι, &c. p. 291.

† Vid. Euseb. de Præp. Evan. ubi. sup.

be supposed that evil entered in their estimation into his work by *his* appointment or permission *.

We have already seen the Egyptians representing the world under the symbol of an egg, proceeding originally from the Creator of the Universe. This symbol, which it is justly supposed that Orpheus learned from this people; he applied in the judgment of a celebrated ancient, to account for the principles of all things, according to a doctrine which the reader will find explained upon philosophical grounds by that writer †. We may observe in general on these hypotheses, that the idea of a dark night, and a chaos, which are said to have preceded the formation of the world; coincide with the language of scripture, that " darkness was on the face of the deep when the spirit of God moved upon the waters ‡." But we ought to reflect that the mind adopts naturally this notion of original anarchy, as preceding order and beautiful disposition; and that it readily employs superior agency in bringing about this great purpose. Without therefore some particular circumstance, such as that above mentioned, to determine our judgment, or historical evidence which is not easily procured, we

---

* Theogon. ab. init.
† Plut. Oper. v. ii. p. 636, &c. ‡ Genes. i. 2.

cannot be justified in pronouncing, that authors in distant nations borrowed in the earliest ages from each other, merely because an original principle may be common to all.

Of the philosophers of Greece, Thales, and Anaximenes, come first to be considered, as being the most ancient, and conspicuous. Of those, the former assigns water*, and the latter air as the first productive element. The former supports his doctrine by the three following properties of water, which give plausibility to his system. 1. Animal life originates in humidity, as this quality is essential to the seed of all animals. 2. To the same great principle we ascribe vegetable subsistence. Plants derive their beauty as well as their prolific quality from moisture; without which they shrink, and speedily disappear. 3. He observed, that the fire of the sun himself is nourished by the exhalations of which his heat is productive, in the same manner as earth; which participates of the benefit. Upon these grounds he pronounced of water, that it is Αρχη των οντων, the original of all things. It ought to be observed, that Thales is supported in this opinion by Homer, who ascribes the original of all things to the ocean.

Ωκεανος οσπερ γενισις παντεσσι τιτυκται.
Plut. de Placit. Philos. Oper. v. ii. p. 875,

* Plut. de Placit Philos. v. ii. p. 875. Lactan. Lib. ii. c. 9.

It is doubtful whether Thales admitted a mind into his system of the universe: for although Cicero ascribes to him the tenet, "that God was the author of all things"*, yet he seems to contradict this affirmation afterwards, by mentioning Anaxagoras as the first philosopher by whom it was maintained †. The same charge may be brought with justice against Laertius ‡.

Anaximenes, the successor of Thales, taught that air, which is infinite, is the cause of all things, being that from which the Gods themselves originally sprang §. Motion as well as matter he held to be eternal. But no intelligent Being is introduced into the great work, either by him or by his predecessor, Anaximander ||.

I have already observed, that Anaxagoras, the scholar of the last mentioned philosopher, was the first who admitted the agency of a pure spirit into his system of the formation of things ¶. In this scheme, which is more consonant than

---

* De Nat. Deor. l. i. cap. 10.
† Id. ibid. ‡ Laert. Anaxag. and Thal.
§ Aug. de Civit. Dei, l. viii. c. 2.
|| Plut. de placit. Philos. Lib. i. c. 3.
¶ Diogen. Laert. Anaxag. Lib. ii. ab. init. Aristot. Oper. v. i. p. 319, 620. Platon. Phæd. p. 72. Aug. de Civit. Dei, Lib. iii. cap. 2.

either of the former to that of revelation, it ought to be remarked, that the Being who superintends all things, is introduced, not as the creator, but as the first mover of parts, which, without his influence, would have been for ever at rest *. The same objection therefore lies against his doctrine, as against that of his successors; the admission of an eternal matter, which existed independently of the first cause, who, upon his hypothesis, is only the principle of motion.

It is astonishing, that the atomic philosophy, founded upon circumstances that are so opposite to the simplest laws of nature, and to those that are most easily comprehended, should have been adopted by names of great eminence, and maintained among the most intelligent people of the world during a succession of ages. That atoms endowed merely with the three qualities, of figure, magnitude, and weight, should have framed the world in its present state fortuitously, after innumerable jostlings, and combinations, is an hypothesis, which it would seem that reason should reject as untenable as soon as it is mentioned. And I consider as one of the clearest

* Αποδιδωσι δε αμφω τη αυτη Αρχη, το τε γινοσκειν και το κινειν; λεγων ΝΟΥΝ κινησαι ΤΟ ΠΑΝ. Aristot. de Anim. Oper. v. i. p. 620.

proofs

proofs of the necessity of revelation, that notions so replete with absurdity obtained credit among the wise, and the learned, as a scheme whereby the science of cosmogony might be explained in a satisfactory manner, to a well informed understanding *.

I cannot agree with those philosophers, (and particularly with the learned and judicious Cudworth;) who would persuade us that Pythagoras was acquainted with the atomical system, and that his Monads are in fact the atoms of Epicurus; because I find such descriptions of the majesty and perfections of God ascribed to him as are irreconcilable to this belief †. Whether this celebrated philosopher understood by the term Monad, GOD, as is generally believed, as the great original of all things; and by the epithet Dyad, an evil ‡, a passive §, or an indefinite prin-

---

* Leucippus is commonly considered as the author of the atomical philosophy. He was followed by Democritus, Epicurus, Strato, Lucretius, &c. of whom the principal person, Epicurus, gained more followers, and obtained greater honours, than any antient philosopher with whom we are acquainted; a circumstance, which, when we consider the absurdity of his tenets, powerfully evinces the necessity of revelation.

† Vid. Clem. Alexan. Stromat. Lib. iv. p. 477. Plut. in Numa. p. 65. Hieron. Præfat. in aur. car. Laert. Pythag. l. 12.

‡ Plutarch. de Placit. Philos. l. i. c. 7. § Id. c. 3.

ciple;

ciple*; it is acknowledged that his followers Ocellus Lucanus, and Philolaus, believed that the world was eternal. And although there be some reason to judge, that they differed in maintaining this tenet from their master; yet, as we are left to collect his opinion of it from succeeding writers, no certain knowledge can be obtained of his genuine doctrine.

Without enlarging on the hypothesis of Zeno, which is encumbered with the same difficulties as those already mentioned †; I now proceed to examine the Platonic account of the creation of the world, and of the departments that are occupied by the persons who framed, and who preside over it. In order to attain these purposes, it is proper that a summary of our author's general doctrine on the formation of the universe, should precede

---

* Dacier Vie de Pythag. and Porphyr. in Vita Pythag.

† A great part of the difficulties wherein the followers of Zeno found themselves involved, in accounting for the various phænomena of the universe, arose from the idea of a corporeal God, or eternal matter animated by the Anima Mundi, whose nature and offices will fall afterwards to be examined. Vid. Senec. Natur. Quest. Lib. ii. c. 45. where he writes concerning God in the following terms: Vis illum vocari mundum? Non falleris. Ipse enim est totum quod vides, totus suis partibus inditus, & se sustinens vi sua. Vid. et. Laert. Zeno, and Cicer. de Nat. Deor. Lib. ii.

an examination of tenets that are properly Platonic, and therefore require illustration.

1. A late ingenious writer observes justly concerning Plato, that no man who considers his definition of *creation* will deny that he had a suitable idea of it. " God, he says, is that Being who confers existence on objects that were formerly unanimated." This writer's words seem to me to be afterwards unintelligible, when he considers matter as an eternal production: for whatever is created, must have had a beginning; and to mention what is eternally created, is an absurdity of the same kind, as to talk of what is immutably fluctuating *.

The opinion of our great philosopher, that spirit existed before matter was produced, and the consequence arising from it respecting the creation of the latter, have already been mentioned. This circumstance alone is surely decisive of the present question: for the belief of the eternity of matter cannot be imputed to that man, who

* Ποιητικην πασαν εφαμεν ειναι δυναμιν, ητις αν αιτια γιγνηται τοις μη προτερον ουσιν, υστερον γιγνεσθαι. Sophist. as quoted by Mr. Ramsay in his Theologie Ancienne. The observation of this author is in these words: La matiere selon lui n'etoit eternelle, que parcequ'elle *etoit produite de tous tems*. And he afterwards considers it not comme une emanation de sa substance, mais comme une veritable production.

maintains that it was preceded by a Being of su-. perior order. This immense and incomprehensible intelligence, who existed eternally himself without generation*, determined to create the universe at an appointed time; and carried his purpose into execution †. He framed heaven, earth, and the inferior deities ‡; and as he fashioned, he pervades all nature, being present at once in heaven, earth, and hell, which are filled by the infinitude of his essence §. Time, which had no being before the work of creation, originated at this period, when it became a mutable image (χυητον τινα αιωνος, as our author terms it) of duration, consisting of days, and months, and years; and containing the past and the future, which make no part of eternity ‖.

Such is our author's general account of the creation of all things; an account so consonant to that of scripture, that we may consider it as a comment on the words of Moses: " in the beginning God created heaven and earth." He who contemplates this sketch of the Platonic doctrines on the present subject, brought into one point of view, and compared with the schemes of former, or of succeeding philosophers, will ac-

---

* Ramsay's Theol. Ancien. p. 44.
† Tim. p. 1046.   ‡ Ibid. p. 1055.
§ De Repub. Lib. x. p. 749.   ‖ Tim. p. 1051.

knowledge

knowledge the justice of Cicero's distinction, when he denominates the God of Plato the maker, and that of Aristotle, the governor of the universe *.

Thus far I have proceeded on plain ground, in explaining the various parts of the Platonic theory of creation. But I should do injustice to my author, by omitting to enter into the more intricate part of his scheme, and to examine particularly the nature of that Being, by whom this great work is said to be accomplished. I shall lay before the reader, in the subsequent part of this section, what appears to me as the genuine doctrine of Plato on this subject; and on those concomitant points which are connected with it, and form principal parts of his theology.

2. It is a circumstance not easily to be accounted for, that the most ancient nations should have conceived the idea of *three persons* as being interested in the creation, and government of the universe; and having spheres assigned to them that are distinct, and independent. Yet it has formerly been evinced, that the Osiris, Isis, and Typhon of the Egyptians are of this nature; al-

* Possumusne dubitare quin mundo præest aliquis *effector* ut Platoni videtur, vel *moderator* tanti operis ut Aristoteli placet. Cicer. Tuscul. Quest. Lib. i.

, though we cannot with certainty trace the original cause of their belief*. Even Zoroaster admitted a mediating power, between his good, and evil principle; and instituted rites, and ceremonies, by the performance of which his followers might at all times conciliate her favour †.

In the writings of Plato, I do not find that three persons are either separately enumerated in succession as occupying various departments, or that they are distinguished as being united in one work, by any common appellation, unless in one passage, which will immediately be quoted. We must therefore collect his ideas of this union, not from the writings of his followers, Proclus, Porphyry, &c. who are explicit in ascribing to their master the belief of a trinity; but from declarations in various parts of his disquisitions, which throw some light on his notions of this *esoteric* and mysterious dogma.

That Plato had formed some idea of a trinity, we might have inferred from an affirmation that is indeed professedly enigmatical; although he had not afterwards specified the persons who

---

* Sect. i. p. 8, &c.

† Προσαπεφαινετο—Μεσον αμφοιν την ΜΙΘΡΗΝ ειναι. Διο δε Μιθρην περσαι την ΜΕΣΙΤΗΝ ονομαζεσιν Εδιδαξε μεν τω ευκταια θυειν και χαριστηρια. Plut. de Isid. and Osirid. Oper. v ii. p.

compose

compose it. The words to which I refer are in his second letter to Dionysius, apparently written in answer to one in which he had been required to give a more explicit account than his former letter had contained, of the nature of God. After having said, that he meant to wrap up his meaning in such obscurity, as that an adept only should fully comprehend it; he adds expressions to the following import: " The Lord of Nature is surrounded on all sides by his works: whatever is, exists by his permission: he is the fountain, and source of excellence: around the second person are placed things of the second order; and around the third, those of the third degree *."

Of this obscure passage, I acknowledge that we can only conjecture the full purport, which I shall afterwards endeavour in some measure to elucidate. At present, it is sufficient to observe, that there is in it an obvious distinction of persons, who are separated in the last part of the sentence; although they appear to be joined by the epithet βασιλεα, (King, or Ruler,) in the first.

From the general consideration of a *Triad* in the divine mind, (if I may thus express it,) I

---

* Περι των παντων βασιλεα, παντ'ιςι, και Εκεινου ενεκα παντα. Εκεινος αιτια παντων των καλων. Δευτερον δε περι τα δευτερα, και τριτον περι τα τριτα. Oper. p. 1269.

now proceed to examine a surer evidence of our author's knowledge of this tenet, arising from the departments which they are represented to occupy.

Of the three persons then, the first, who is distinguished particularly by the appellation ΠΑΤΗΡ, Father*, is the ΤΟ ΕΝ of whom we have already seen, that Plato writes in terms the most sublime, and appropriate; the ΘΕΟΣ strictly so called, in whose unsearchable *essence* that of all other Beings is absorbed, and comprehended. His second person is the ΔΗΜΙΟΥΡΓΟΣ, or ΛΟΓΟΣ, to whom, as we shall see immediately, the work of creation is particularly assigned by Plato, as it is by the Evangelist. With these is conjoined the ΨΥΧΗ του ΚΟΣΜΟΥ, or soul of the world, as the peculiar cause of the preservation of animal, and vegetable life. I shall make a few observations at present, on the nature and offices of the two latter persons; of whom the departments bear a particular relation to the present subject.

That Plato considers the second person of his Triad, as having presided at the work of creation, is obvious from a passage of his Epinomis, of which the mode of expression is remarkably sig-

---

* Τον των παντων Θεον, Ηγεμονων τε οντων και των μελλοντων; τη τε Ηγεμονος και Αιτιου ΠΑΤΕΡΑ, και ΚΥΡΙΟΝ επομνυντας. Plat. Epist. 7.

nificant.

nificant. "The ΛΟΓΟΣ, the WORD, he says, divine above all other Beings, fashioned and rendered the heavenly bodies conspicuous in their various revolutions. This Being, an happy man, will principally reverence, while he may be stimulated by the desire of learning, whatever is within the compass of human understanding: being convinced, that he will thus enjoy the greatest felicity in this life; and that after death, he will be translated into regions that are congenial (προσηκοντα) to virtue *."

By the term ΛΟΓΟΣ in this sentence, I should be inclined to understand nothing more than the command, or word of the great Creator, which, no doubt, is its most obvious import †, were it

not

---

* Ον εταξε ΛΟΓΟΣ ο ΠΑΝΤΩΝ ΘΕΙΟΤΑΤΟΣ, ορατον, ον ο μεν ευδαιμων πρωτον μεν θαυμασειν· Επειτα δε ερωτα ισχει τε καταμασθειν επασα θνητει φυσει δυνατα· υγεμενος αριστ ουτως ευτυχεστατα τη διαξειν του σιον τελευτησας τε προς τοπες εξειν προσηκοντας αρετη. Platon. Oper. p. 1011, 12.

† A learned author of the present age is of opinion, that "the translators of the New Testament were mistaken in rendering ΛΟΤΟΣ in the beginning of St. John's Gospel, by WORD, which to *him* conveys no meaning at all. For how can I understand, he says, that *word*, that is to say, speech, or ideas expressed by articulation, is GOD?" Origin of Language, v. i. p. 7. I do not see, that the Christian doctrine of the trinity would be injured by admitting this author's explanation of it, as Λογος ενδιαθετος, i. e. reason in

the

not that the following circumstances seem to evince, that it hath here a more particular signification.

the mind of the Deity. But his ingenuity will perhaps reject as a frigid criticism his remark on the term ΛΟΓΟΣ, as improperly applied to denote the second person of the trinity, because it signifies speech, when it suggests to him, that this articulate voice is the mean by which God is represented to have framed the universe. " He spake, and it was done: he commanded, and it was brought to pass." The substitution therefore of the FIAT of the Creator, for the Being who pronounced it, is a licence which neither requires an apology, nor exceeds comprehension. No man, while he contemplates the image which it places before his imagination, will find its energy impaired by the recollection of the grammatical import of the term; or will judge that it is applied with less propriety, beauty, and significance, to denote the power of the Being who presided at this work, than A and Ω, (the first and last letters of the Greek alphabet,) are to express his pre-existence, and duration. Our author himself seems indeed to have forgotten what he here says on the sense of the term ΛΟΓΟΣ, in a subsequent part of his work, wherein are the following words, " ΛΟΓΟΣ in its proper signification, denotes comparison, though it is *commonly* used to denote *all the operations of intellect*, and even *intellect itself.*" Origin of Lang. v. i. p. 109. N. Now if we adhere in translating the words of the Evangelist, to the common import of the term in this writer's estimation, their literal meaning is that which follows: " In the beginning was mind, or intellectual operation. And mind was with God: and mind was God, &c." St. John, ch. i. v. 1. Thus in whatever acceptation we understand this term, the sense of our translation seems to be that of the Evangelist.

1. The

1. The ΛΟΓΟΣ here mentioned by Plato, is not a thing, but a person, who is held forth in this character, in the detail of a great transaction. In the first sentence, he is the Maker of the Universe: in the following one, the epithet ὅν is applied to him, in order to shew that the personification is preserved; and happiness is said to be found in supreme admiration of his perfections.

2. I do not find, that the epithet above mentioned is applied in any part of our author's writings, to signify the first, and original cause of all things. It must therefore characterize some other Being, who is distinguished from the former.

3. It appears from a passage of a letter written by Plato to his three friends, Erastus, Hermias, and Coriscus, that he had framed an idea of the difference between the paternal and filial character of the God-head: and as we have already seen, that the term ΛΟΓΟΣ is never applied to denominate the former, the latter acceptation is that which most properly belongs to it. His words are, "You ought to repeat the words of this letter frequently among yourselves, invoking GOD, the supreme director of all present and future events, and the Father, and Lord of this director *."

* See the original in p. 39.

When

When we add to these observations, that the prosopopeia occurs more frequently in the writings of our great philosopher, than in those perhaps of any other author, we have laid a foundation on which we may establish the following conclusion; that the ΛΟΓΟΣ is not only personified in the present case, but that this term hath the same import in the work of the Heathen, as in that of the Evangelist; and is applied in both to denote the second person of the God-head.

I come now to a branch of my subject, in explaining the natural offices of the third person of the Platonic Triad, the Anima Mundi; on which many comments have been made, and many conjectures offered, by ancient and modern theologists. It may perhaps be a doubtful question, whether Plato was or was not the original author of this celebrated dogma: but be that matter as it may, no man who is acquainted with his writings will hesitate to acknowledge, that it is explained and illustrated at greater length by him, than by any of his predecessors among the ancients. As an introduction to the account which I propose to give of our author's doctrine on this head, and to the hypotheses of his numerous commentators, it will here be proper to examine his principles concerning the formation of the universe, and the materials of which it was framed.

I have

I have already endeavoured to refute the charge that is brought against our great philosopher, as having maintained the eternity of matter. I shall add only farther, for the satisfaction of those who may demand particular proof of his doctrine, that his writings abound with declarations on the present subject, of which the meaning cannot be misapprehended. With this purpose he denominates at one time, the principles or substance of all things, Γενοματα Θεον Δημιουργον, the productions of the efficient Deity*; and at others enters more particularly into the question. Thus he observes, that many persons are ignorant of the nature and power of mind or intellect, "as having existed at the beginning, *antecedent to all bodies* †." Of this mind, he observes, that it is without exception Παντων πρεσβυτατη, "*of all things* the most ancient ‡:" and he subjoins, in order to remove all doubt of his purpose, that it is also Αρχη κινησεως, "the cause or principle of motion §."

Assuming

---

* Plat. Sophist.

† Εν πρωτοις εστι Σωματων εμπροσθεν παντων γενομενη. De Legib. Lib. x. p. 952.

‡ Id. ibid.

§ This tenet of Plato will be found upon examination to throw considerable light on an important part of his philosophy. The censure of Aristotle, and his preference of the scheme of Anaxagoras, who taught that the particles of the first matter were at rest, to that of our author, in whose

plan

Assuming then as a truth, the proposition, that matter in the estimation of Plato, was preceded by spirit, to which it owes its original, let us proceed to examine the constituent parts of the universe according to his philosophy, and the plan they are agitated; and his reasoning in defence of it, would have been superseded by recollecting, that the *motion* of these particles or atoms is ascribed by Plato *to the spirit who produced them*; and who is therefore denominated in the words immediately quoted, Αρχη Κινησεως. He would have discovered by attention to this circumstance, that the schemes of both philosophers ultimately coincide, and would have avoided the making an imaginary distinction. Plutarch, whether misled by this author, or from inattention to the doctrine of Plato, falls into the same errors, and represents the principle of Anaxagoras, that all bodies were at rest until the period at which he says, ΝΟΥΝ Κινησαι το παν, that *mind* moved the universe, as opposite to our author's maxim, who maintains, that the matter of the chaos had an original disorderly motion. But let the intelligent reader find out if he can, the distinction between the ΝΟΥΣ of Anaxagoras, who is said to have moved the elements that were at rest, and the ΨΥΧΗ of Plato, who is ΑΡΧΗ ΚΙΝΗΣΕΩΣ, the original of motion in these elements. If he can discover any difference of opinion between philosophers who establish this principle, in the consequence that results from it, I must have misapprehended their purpose. But, if according to both theories, rest must have preceded the motion which MIND communicated to the first matter, observations that are built on another foundation must fall to the ground. Vid. Aristot. de Cælo, Lib. iii. c. 7. Plutarch. de placit. Philos. Lib. i. c. 7. This distinction is strenuously maintained by Bayle. Dict. Crit. Art. Anaxag. Rem. C.

laws by which the Deity appears to have regulated its natural government.

Before the period at which the omnific word brought order and harmony into its works, the four elements, whereof all bodies are compounded, were jumbled together, according to all the ancients who preceded Plato, in a chaos, or crude mass of the originals of things. The great point therefore which they studied to determine, was, not whether the world had an original, but of what substance it was framed. Without entering into the various theories of philosophers on this subject, of which the principal were formerly enumerated, I observe only at present, that our author's hypothesis hath in one essential respect the advantage of those of his predecessors. For while they ascribe to one original element, or principle, the production of bodies, his doctrine, which comprehends the rudiments of all taken together, rests upon a broader and more adequate foundation.

Of this nature is the ΥΛΗ, or first matter of our great philosopher. It is principally in the Timæus, that we find an account of this original substance. I shall lay before the reader as much of his description as is necessary to the present purpose.

The ΥΛΗ, of which the universe was framed, without coming under the designation of any element, contains, according to Timæus, the seeds or principles of all. It is on this account that he terms it the original genus of all things *. In its original state, after having been framed by the Supreme Mind, the parts of this mass were confused, conformed, and agitated during some time in various convolutions; until the first mover, directing the fluctuation to a particular end, interposed more immediately to bring order out of confusion †.

The first elements which God separated from chaos in order to frame the world, were those of fire and earth. These elements had precedency of the others, because corporeal objects must be rendered visible and tangible: and to have the former quality, they must participate of fire; as they receive the latter, by being compounded of matter. But it is according to Timæus, with bodies that are fashioned of different substances, as with distinct numbers or quantities, of which two are united by an intermediate mean, that bears an equal relation to both. As earth and fire are solids which have depth as well as extent, and can only be brought to cohere in one mass,

---

* Γɩνος εξʋ ΤΟ ΠΑΝ συνετιθη. Tim.
† Id. Plat. Oper. p. 1047.

by the aid of two such mediums, the Supreme Being therefore created *air* and *water*. These, by intermixing with the first elements, and by facilitating at the same time that they perfect their coalition, render the world a compact and dense body, that is neither injured by accident, nor subjected to decay *.

But by what means it will be asked, are elements apparently so discordant and hostile to each other, brought to coalesce so perfectly into a common mass or stratam, as to promote beneficial instead of producing destructive effects?

In reply to this question, Plato, in the character of a cosmogonist, considers the forms of the constituent parts of matter, and attempts to analise its modifications. Of the four elements that enter into this substance, he observes, that three are peculiarly fitted by the triangular form of their parts, which are volatile and fluctuating, to operate in the fourth, a fixed and solid substance, constructed of cubical particles, to which heat, air, and motion, give at the same time stability and animation. Our author's theory of fire in this enumeration, is particularly curious. It consists, he tells us, of acute pyramidical parts, whose triangular sides, and penetrating

* Tim. p. 1048, 49.

points,

points, are calculated to enter into all other bodies; of which this singular conformation dissolves the original disposition. We must ascribe to the power of this all-pervading element, originating perhaps in the cause above mentioned, that it became in early ages a peculiar object of religious adoration *.

Having followed our author in his account of the constituent forms and structure of the universe, we are naturally led to consider in the third person of the Platonic Triad, the Being, to whom, as the source of universal animation, Plato gives the peculiar designation, Ψυχη του κοσμου, or soul of the world.

This governing spirit, of whom the earth, properly so called, is the body, consisted, according to our author's philosophy, of the same and the other; that is, of the first matter, and of pure intelligence, framed to actuate the machinery of nature. The Supreme Being, after having created, placed him in the middle of the earth, which, in the vivid idea of Plato, seemed itself to live, in consequence of an influence that was felt in every part of it. From this seat his power is represented as being extended on all sides to the utmost limit of the heavens; con-

* Tim. p. 1049, &c.

ferring

ferring life, and preserving harmony in the various and complicated parts of the universe*. Upon this Being God is said to have looked with peculiar complacency after having created him as an image of himself, and to have given beauty and perfect proportion to the mansion which he was destined to occupy.

From the observations that have been made on this dogma, the reader will perceive, that the earth in Plato's estimation, is a *living animal*, informed as the human body, by a spirit, whose influence is felt in every part of it, and who acts

---

* Tim. and De Legib. Lib. x. p. 952. and Ciceron, Oper. v. iv. p. 595. Plut. Tim. Oper. v. 2. Aristotle (who does not always succeed in censuring his master,) attempts to prove, in opposition to the doctrine of Timæus, that the world which had no beginning, will have no termination: and he finds fault with our author for asserting, that the universe, although it was created by God, may yet remain for ever incorruptible. Oper. v. i p. 450. But this affirmation is certainly unsupported by argument. For although we should acknowledge the truth of the proposition, that what had no original will never have an end; it will not follow from this concession, that what had a beginning must *therefore* have a period. The preservation of the world from corruption, or decay, depends not upon the circumstance of its having originated, but upon the power of the Being by whom it was produced, to prevent anarchy, or corruption, from taking place in his workmanship. And no man will deny, that he who framed the structure of the universe, is equal to the task of preventing its dissolution.

in subserviency to the ends of his creation. In order to facilitate the operation of this intelligence, the form of the earth is perfectly orbicular*, a shape of which the extremities that are in all parts equidistant from the centre, become susceptible in the same degree of an influence that is felt from this point, throughout the body. According to the doctrine of Timæus, the Supreme Being struck out from this original mind, innumerable spirits of inferior order, endowed with principles of reason; and he committed to Divinities of secondary rank the task of investing these in material forms, and of dispersing them as inhabitants of the sun, moon, and other celestial bodies. He taught also, that at death the human soul is reunited to the Ψυχη του Κοσμου, as to the source from which it originally came.

Such is the third person of the Platonic Triad, in the writings of our great philosopher. Let us now contemplate this Being in the comments of his disciples. I select on this head the four

* Plato terms it σφαιροιδις, and adds, that nothing can be more perfectly circular than its form. The true figure of the globe, is an oblate spheroid, projected at the equator, and flatted at the poles by its diurnal rotation on its own axis; and the causes of this inequality were unknown to our author, with whose theory they do not perfectly correspond. Tim. ubi supra.

following

following hypotheses, as the principal of those to which the present subject has given occasion. An enlargement on them at considerable length, would be inconsistent with the professed purpose of these observations.

1. By the soul of the world, some writers understand, that igneous and animating breath, which was infused into the chaos, in order to introduce symmetry and proportion into the work of the Deity. They found their notion upon the Πυρ ανωμαλοτατον δημιυργον of Plato, which Virgil seems to have had in view, when mentioning the heavenly bodies, he says,

 Igneus est ollis vigor, & celestis origo seminibus.
          Æneid. Lib. vi.

Zeno, the celebrated founder of the stoical tribe, maintained also this opinion, when he denominated *fire* a fifth element, from which reason and intelligence arose [*].

2. Our author is represented by other philosophers, to understand nothing more by his ruling spirit, than the form and proportion of parts

---

[*] Stoici quatuor ex rebus omnia conetare dicerant. Cum autem quæreretur num Quinta quædam Natura videretur esse, ex qua ratio & intelligentia oriretur?—Zeno id dixit esse *Ign. m.* Ciceron. Oper. Tom. iv. p. 335 and 354.

that are conspicuous in the works of nature, and the elements whereby they are cemented. This is the opinion of his commentator Serranus among others*, and coincides indeed in some measure with the doctrine of Timæus, who defines the *soul* of the world by the terms, Αναλογια και Συμμετρια, analogy and symmetry,-in opposition to the *body*, which he terms αρατον και απτον, visible and tangible. If, by those epithets thus applied, it be supposed that Plato understood the harmonious concurrence of different mental powers in producing a certain end, I know not that any objection can lie against this acceptation. But if the purpose be, to refine away the sense of the whole doctrine, by insinuating that our author holds forth an allegorical person in his Ψυχη του κοσμου, nothing can be more opposite to the spirit of his philosophy, or more irreconcilable to the most explicit declaration. We have already seen that this governing intelligence is said by Plato to be the first or eldest of all Beings; that he is denominated the principle of motion; that his influence is universally extended, and that he was contemplated by the Being who framed him with complacency and pleasure. In the judgment of the great Roman philosopher, this spirit is a Mind, or Divinity,

* Gale's Court of the Gent. P. II. Book ix. p. 324. &c. Aug. de Civit. Dei, l. xii. c. 5.

who

who is invested by the earth, as by a body; and is placed in the middle of it, as the place that is best adapted to his operation. He is embraced by the vast concave of heaven, wherein he expatiates without embarrassment, or controul *.

3. In the last quoted passage, Cicero mentions the third, and most common acceptation of the Ψυχη του κοσμου, as a soul that actuates the external orb of the world, in the same manner as the human mind animates every part of the body that is assigned to it; and promotes its own purposes by the instrumentality of the organs of sense.

> Principio, cœlum, & terras, camposque liquentes,
> Lucentemque globum Lunæ, titaniaque astra
> Spiritus intus alit, totosque infusa per artus,
> MENS agitat molem.
> Æneid. Lib. vi.

This sense of the term is that which Plato himself appears to have adopted in the passages above mentioned: and it is not therefore necessary that I should enlarge at length on the corresponding sentiments of his later followers and commentators.

---

* Animum in ejus (terræ) medium collocavit, ita per totum tetendit: deinde eum circumdedit corpore, & vestivit extrinsecus; cœloque solivago & volubili, & in orbem incitato complexus est. Cicer. Oper. v. iv. p. 595.

4. From

4. From the offices wherein this spirit is said to be occupied, and from his perfect resemblance of the first cause, Christian writers, of much erudition, have laboured in proving that our intelligent philosopher had received by tradition some idea of the third person of the trinity; and that the Ψυχη του κοσμου of Timæus, is the spirit of the Jewish legislator, who is said to have moved on the face of the waters*. These authors quote two passages of scripture in defence of their hypothesis wherein this doctrine seems to be inculcated. One is in Job, who in the 4th verse of his 33d chapter, ascribes his own creation and preservation to the spirit of God: the other is the 30th verse of the 104th Psalm, where this Divine Being is said to be the efficient of the universe, and the cause of its renovation.

Of those ingenious comments on the text of Plato, we may pronounce without hesitation, that the two former, and the latter, contain some part of his doctrine, without however placing a compleat view of it before the mind. His genuine sense of the subject is exhibited under the third division, and has been already explained. It is only farther requisite, in order to confirm the preceding observations, that after

---

* Vid. Ludov. Viv. Comment. Aug. de Civit. Dei, l. x, c. 23. Gale's Court of the Gent. B. III. ch. ix. p. 323.

having

having thus endeavoured to illustrate the true doctrine of Plato on the present topic, we should follow his soul of the world, in obtaining a compleat idea of the nature and offices of this governing spirit, in his various spheres of operation.

According to our author's theory, this Being, of whom we have already seen the origin and place of residence, is employed in the two great departments of physical and moral government. Let us examine his peculiar office both in the former and latter province.

1. It is with the purpose of marking the influence of his universal spirit on the globe which we inhabit, that Plato denominates this mass of animated matter ζων εμψυχον και εννουν*, "a Being endowed with life and intelligence," wherein mind is conspicuously predominant. The first principle of life and motion in the body of this animal, is spirit, as has already been shewn. This ethereal substance, agitating, pervading, and invigorating all the parts of nature †, is that fire which penetrates the pores of all bodies, and thus becomes the cause of vegetative life: his

---

* Tim. ubi supra, p. 4.
† Plato calls him ψυχη διοικουσα και—βοικουσα εν απασι. De Legib. Lib. x. p. 951.

influence

influence is not less powerfully felt in the solar orb than in our terrestrial region*, wherein he is alternately the Ceres that fructifies the earth, and the Neptune who agitates the ocean: by his breath therefore nature is prevented from languishing in her operations, or from sinking at last under the ruin of an edifice which time is perpetually undermining: finally, the concurrence of all these circumstances renders him, in our author's estimation, a GOD by whom life is preserved in all animals †.

2. While the Supreme Being accomplishes such important ends by the ministration of this spirit in the natural world, he is not less attentive in effecting by his means, the great purposes of moral government. Our author had, without doubt, this sphere of operation in view, when he represents his third person of his Triad, as the ruling as well as the animating principle; who renders the passions, opinions, and prejudices of men alternately subservient to the great purpose of general felicity ‡, as much as the
successive

---

* Ηλιον ιωπερ αγει Ψυχη, &c. ibid.

† Tim. p. 1052, and De Legib. Lib. x. ubi sup. Plutarch, in his summary of the Platonic doctrines, observes in the same spirit, Ο ΘΕΟΣ Νευ; ιτι του κοσμου. De placit. Phil. Oper. v. ii. p. 878.

‡ Αγη μεν δε Ψυχη παντα τα κατ Ουρανον και γην, και θαλασσαν,
τα.;

successive changes of heat, and cold, tempest, and sunshine; changes, that contribute in the course of providence, to preserve an order of which they are apparently subversive. On other occasions, Plato applies the term ΝΟΥΣ, mind, as well as ΘΕΟΣ to this universal agent; and he assigns as the reason of naming the universe a living animal, that its government is under his direction *.

Thus I have endeavoured to make the reader acquainted with the theories of the most eminent ancients, and particularly with the doctrines of Plato, on a theme, which they appear to have considered as deeply interesting, and important. I have been solicitous in explaining the philosophy of the latter on this subject, to illustrate the obscurity of the passage that was quoted when I entered into it; of which the meaning is professedly enigmatical, and involved. It is obvious, that our author assigns in that passage, distinct spheres as appropriated to the persons of his triad; suited at the same time to their natures, and to the order wherein they are placed. We may now consider with a clear comprehen-

---

ταις αυτης κινησισιν, αις ονοματα ϵισιν βουλισθαι, σκοπϵισθαι, &c. Πασιν οις Ψυχη χρωμϵνη Νουν μϵν προς λαμβανουσα, αϵι Θϵιον Θϵος ουσα, ορθα και ϵυδαιμονα πϵδαγωγϵι παντα. Oper. p. 952, 53.

* Id. ibid.

sion

sion of the Platonic doctrine, those persons as occupying their various departments.

I have already rendered evident, that by the βασιλεα, the King, whom Plato distinguishes as his first person, he understands the το ον, the self-existing and eternal principle by whom the first matter was originally created. This is the Being, whom, as I shall afterwards endeavour to evince, our author elsewhere denominates Saturn. He is held forth in the character of universal Father, as surrounded by all subordinate intelligences, who wait to execute his commands: and as the first and best of Beings, he is said to have prevented the admission of evil into the system of nature, during the happy period of his administration *.

The Θεος Δημιυργος is distinguished with great beauty and propriety by the term λογος, as being the instrument by whom the eternal Father created all things; and to whose word or fiat, a corresponding energy was therefore communicated. When the το εν having resigned for a time the reins of government, retired *into the contemplation of himself* †; we must suppose that

---

* Polit. Oper. 537.
† The words of Plato are, τοτε δε τε παντος ο μεν κυϐερνητης, πηδαλιων οιακος αφεμενος, εις ΤΗΝ ΑΥΤΟΥ ΠΕΡΙΩΠΗΝ απεϛη. p. 538.

this person assumed the reins as the representative of his Father*: and although evil hath not been wholly repelled by him, it is yet at all times said to be opposite to his nature, and to have had a necessary and independent original. The various revolutions therefore which are the subjects of history, as well as events, of more immediate importance to individuals, are conducted by this universal Ruler, who will retain the dominion wherewith he is invested, until the Father, at an appointed season, will reassume his authority; and having restored harmony, and beautiful order to the universe, will put an end for ever to old age, and death.

That the third person of the Platonic Triad, the Ψυχη του κοσμου, is distinct from the two former, and that he occupies a separate department, will be acknowledged; when we consider in one point of view the circumstances on which we have formerly enlarged: that the body wherewith he is invested had an original; that he is said to be compounded as man, of matter and spirit; that

---

* This is obviously the sense of our author in the words formerly quoted, wherein the Δημιυργος is said to be παντων θιος, Ηγιμων των τι οντων και μιλλοντων. Plato, (as we shall see more particularly afterwards;) not only specifies the time at which this reign commenced, but determines also the period when the second person will deliver up the kingdom to the Father. Polit. ubi sup.

his

his influence must be limited in duration; and, finally, that the sphere of his operation is inferior and subordinate. Cicero was most probably influenced by these considerations in forming his opinion of the Anima Mundi, whom he not only pronounces to have been produced by the Author of Nature for particular purposes, but to act at all times in obedience to his direction *.

I have now attempted to execute one principal purpose of the present section, in the illustration of an obscure and mysterious dogma, that has the most important truths as its objects: and the observations that have been made on it will have their proper effect, if the learned reader should find that they throw some light on the tenet formerly mentioned. "*The Lord of Nature is surrounded on all sides by his works: whatever is, exists by his permission: around the second person are placed things of the second order; and around the third, are those of the third degree.*"

I cannot conclude this section without remarking, as an inference arising from the pre-

* Sic Deus ille eternus hunc perfecte beatum Deum procreavit: sed animum haud ita cum corpus effecisset, inchoavit: neque enim esset rectum *minorem* parere *majorem*. Ciceron. Oper. v. iv. p. 595.

ceding

ceding illustration, that the doctrine of the ancients in general, as well as of Plato in particular, on the well-known subject of a Triad, is somewhat different from that of the gospel, to which it has apparent similarity. The Godhead, indeed, consists according to their united declarations, of three persons, who have distinct employments and departments. But I have endeavoured to evince beyond question, that the appellation ΤΟ ΕΝ is applied by our author immediately to the first person, as excluding equality, or competition. HE is the ΘΕΟΣ *properly so called*, as distinguished from the ΘΕΟΣ ΔΗΜΙΟΥΡΓΟΣ, or ΨΥΧΗ τȣ κοσμȣ. The sublime mystery of the Trinity, as it was revealed to the inspired writers, is unquestionably more consonant to the divine nature and perfections, than the theory of unenlightened philosophers, on a subject that exceeds comprehension. While therefore we receive the former with reverence and gratitude, as revealed with the best purpose, and established by the highest authority, we may perceive with emolument, in contemplating the latter, how nearly the notions which fallible men conceived of this doctrine, coincided with the testimony of writers, who were commissioned to promulgate it to mankind.

SECTION III.

INHABITANTS OF THE AIR, AND ELEMENTS. FORMATION, AND CONSTITUENT PRINCIPLES OF MAN.

IN an examination of the various orders and departments of Pagan divinities, the beings of middle rank, who may be said to fill up in some degree the immense chasm between the divine and human nature, form curious and interesting objects of speculation. I propose in the present section, to lay before the reader the doctrine of the ancients concerning the nature and offices of those beings, who, in their estimation, were immediate agents in the government of the universe; as it is essentially connected with the Platonic theory of the origin, and constituent principles of man. It is proper only to observe, before I enter upon the subject, that as our author's account of it does not differ materially from that of other philosophers, although it be far more comprehensive and accurate, I shall treat the doctrine at large, without making any particular distinction.

In whatever light we regard the belief of an intermediate race of beings, a reflecting mind will

will consider it as having originated in notions which men conceived at a very early period, of the perfection of the Supreme Mind, and of their own comparative weakness and impurity. Of these they perceived without difficulty, that the former rendered them unable, and the latter unworthy, to prefer their requests immediately to a Being, who is at the same time perfectly good, and universally intelligent. And, in fact, nothing is more terrible to a heart that is conscious of fatal propensities, whereof it can neither resist the influence, nor efface the impressions, than the sense of dependence upon an universal ruler, whose discernment is the witness of crimes, which justice forbids that he should pardon.

From this view therefore of the Deity, and of themselves, men, who trembled in the presence of perfect and uncreated excellence, wished to remove the embarrassment of an approach to it; an approach rendered necessary by exigency and imperfection. Hence, they were led to believe in the existence of a certain middle order of Beings, propitious to the supplications, and compassionate to the frailties of mankind; as being placed between their own nature, and that of perfect intelligence: and to them, as creatures who participated of their own weakness and dependence,

pendence, they found consolation in making known their desires.

But granting it may be said, that we have here assigned the cause to which the doctrine of intermediate orders owed its original, what is the nature of those Beings, and of what kind are the offices wherein their various classes are supposed to be occupied? To these questions, arising naturally from the subject, the following observations are proposed as an answer: and my purpose will be gained, if the learned reader should find in them, some satisfactory account of the point which they are meant to illustrate.

Without entering at once into particular investigation, I consider the Dæmons or Genii, who figure in the theology of the ancients, as being, in general, either of the celestial or terrestrial order. Those of the first rank inhabit the higher, and these of the second the lower region of air: and the exterior form of each class is adapted according to Plato, as we shall see afterwards, to a particular sphere of operation*. Some general remarks on the dæmoniacal character will introduce most naturally those that may be made on each class separately reviewed.

* Epinom. Oper. p. 1011.

Notwithstanding the agreement of ancient writers in believing the existence of Dæmons, to which they were impelled by the motives above mentioned, they differ widely in their accounts of the nature of those beings as distinguished from each other. The points wherein they coincide on this subject are, their acknowledgment that Dæmons had an original, and that their nature is inferior to the *divine*, properly thus denominated*; that it is however superior to that of mankind, whom they excel in power, comprehension, and intelligence †; finally, that by sharing the impassive and immortal nature of the Gods ‡, with the various passions of the human species, they are peculiarly adapted to that middle state which they are destined to occupy §. In other important circumstances concerning these intelligences, it would seem that men had very different opinions. Thus they have been alternately represented, as the souls of wicked men, who retained in their state of separation from the body, the appetites that prevailed in it ‖; as angels originally upright, whose na-

---

* Plutarch. Oper. v. ii. p. 415. † Plat. 1194.

‡ Aug. de Civit. Dei. l. viii. c. 14. p. 484. Plutarch however seems to question their immortality. Oper. v. ii. p. 419.

§ Aug. ubi supra, Laert. Pythag. l. viii. p. 581 and 587.

‖ Joseph.

tures became contaminated by their intercourse with mankind, of whom they were entrusted with the charge*; as spirits who assumed for particular ends, bodies whereof the senses take cognisance †; and finally, as Genii, who having been cast out of heaven, fell upon the earth, the water, and the air, in which they are perpetually exciting commotions ‡.

An inquiry into the nature of the dæmoniacal body, may be said to minister rather to curiosity than to use. It is proper however to give some account of it, as it is connected with other parts of the subject.

In general then, the forms of the Dæmons participated according to the doctrine of the ancients, of their disposition and character; being neither altogether celestial nor corporeal. They consisted of air, not condensed as a cloud that floats on the atmosphere, but so pure, subtile, and rarefied, as not to be perceived by our organs of sight, unless when the superior Being chooses to render himself visible for any par-

---

* Lactan. de Orig. Error. l. ii. c. 15. and Plat. p. 527.

† Lud. Viv. in Aug. de Civit. Dei, v. ii. p. 156. Hence these Beings acquired the name of Incubi, familiar spirits, &c. whom Superstition enlisted as her attendants.

‡ Aug. de Civit, Dei, v. i. l. 10. c. 9.

ticular purpose. He assumes in this case a vehicle of grosser air, whose condensation renders it discernible, and of which the yielding materials are with equal facility collected and dissolved. To bodies thus infinitely subtilised and attenuated, they believed that a pure and uncorrupted aliment was suited by the Creator, as different from that whereby we are supported, as the forms to which it is adapted are from our own *.

These remarks on the nature and general employment of Dæmons, naturally introduce an account of the two great classes into which it was observed that they are divided.

---

* Dæmonum corpora Apuleius medio dicit, inter terrenam & æthereum naturam; multoque minus concreta quam nubes, & longe subtiliora ex purissimo aeris liquido & sereno alimento coalita, &c. Ludov. Viv. Comment. l. viii. c. 15. Plato distinguishes from each other the two great orders of Dæmons, by forms suited to the regions wherein they expatiate. The superior are of pure æther, the inferior of grosser air. Των δε δυο τουτων ζων, τα τ'εξ αιθερος, εφεξης τε αερος, ου διορωμενον ολον αυτων εκατερον τιναι. Epinom. p. 1011. The term ολον in this application obviously implies, that either order of these intelligences might be dimly and partially discerned by spectators. Our author (as we shall see afterwards;) seems to consider this faculty elsewhere, as being principally exercised by the Genii of the waters.

1. Those

1. Those dignified employments, which without respecting a city, or a province, comprehend MAN as their object, are ascribed by the ancients to the superior order of Genii, who are therefore placed in points of view the most conspicuous and attractive. Without entering at length into the various disquisitions of authors on this subject, I mention the following general heads as containing whatever is most worthy of observation.

1. The first and principal office of those spirits, in the opinion of the most intelligent philosophers of antiquity, is, that of mediating, or of performing beneficent offices between God and Man*. Many difficulties, says Plutarch, are solved by those who believe that the Genii occupy a middle department between God and Man, and that they are employed in reconciling and uniting their natures †: and he afterwards considers the loss of the orders of Genii as an event, which by breaking the continuity of things, would make a void in the universe, and put an end to the intercourse between God and his creatures, in the same manner as the dissolution of that body of air which fills up the space between the earth and the moon, would loosen

---

* Vid. Auct. inf. citat.   † Plat. Oper. v. ii. p. 415.

and

and annihilate the bands, whereby unity and coherence are preserved in the system *.

Thales, who taught that all nature was replete with Dæmons †, and Pythagoras, the master of Plato, appear to have coincided in the same opinion of their importance and utility ‡. But our author himself, who seems to have viewed the subject in all its extent, affirms, that God interferes not in human transactions, unless by the mediation of these subordinate Beings, who are alternately employed in the office of transmitting intelligence to the Gods, and to men, of things wherein both are concerned §. It appears according to an author formerly quoted, that the ancient Egyptians and Phrygians concurred in this opinion of the mediation of Genii, which is likewise supposed to have been the doctrine of Orpheus and Zoroaster ‖. The same author joins with Laertius **, in considering this dogma as having been inculcated by Zeno, and the Stoics ††. From those joint authorities we may therefore affirm, that the belief of a middle order of Beings, who mediated

---

* Plut. ubi supra. † Laert. l. xvi. p. 18.
‡ Id. Lib. viii. p. 587. § Plut. p. 1194.
‖ Plut. ubi supra. ** Laert. Zeno.
†† Id. Pythag. p. 587.

between

between the Deity and his rational creatures, was in general prevalent among the ancients.

2. In their particular office of presiding over mankind, these intelligences are the authors of prophecy, and of divination: of the former, by impressing in a supernatural manner the knowledge of futurity upon the thought of the Seer, or Prophet; of the latter, by their attention to sacrifices, wherein the will of the Gods was consulted. In the character of predicting future events, I shall afterwards have occasion to examine the influence which it was believed that Dæmons exerted in producing in many instances the phænomenon of dreaming, when the visions were ascribed to supernatural impulse. At present it sufficeth to observe, that they are peculiarly objects of estimation, when we consider them as having dictated the oracle's responses, whereby the fate of nations was announced*, and influenced magicians in the work of divination †. We cannot have clearer evidence that

---

* It is to this circumstance that Plato most probably alludes when he mentions the διὰ τῶν ϑυσιασμον as one of the branches of divination carried on by the ministration of dæmons.

† The best, and most complete account of the various species of divination, is that of Ludovicus Vives, in his Commentary on Aug. de Civit. Dei. v. i. l. 7. p. 437. See also Gales Court of the Gent. p. 3, 64, &c.

Dæmons were employed in the former office than the testimony of Plutarch, who ascribes the ceasing of oracles to the desertion, extinction, or migration of those Genii who presided in this business *. The magical incantations in the same manner, whereby futurity was developed, were employed in calling up those spirits as the authors of divination †, which Plato considers (I know not for what reason) as tending to promote friendly intercourse between the divine and human nature ‡.

When we consider the busy order of intelligences as peopling all the elements, and presiding at every great transaction that had the future for its object, we are led to view their influence in the rite of sacrifice as having been exerted with peculiar efficacy §. And it is on this account, as we shall see immediately, that they were wor-

---

* Plut. Oper. v. ii. p. 418.
† Philost. Vit. Apollon,
‡ Και εςιν η Μαντικη (says our author) Φιλιας θεων και Ανθρωπων Δημιεργος, τω επισ]οσθαι τα κατα ανθρωπους ερωτικα, οσα τινα προς θεμιν, και ασεβειαν. Sympos.

§ Διο τουτου, και η μαντικη πασα χωρει, και η των ιερων τεχνη, των τε περι τας θυσιας και τας τιλετας και τας επωδας, και την μαντικην πασαν, και γοητειαν. Conviv. ubi sup.

shipped

shipped with ceremonies that indicated religious veneration *.

3. The beings above-mentioned are represented in the execution of their charge over mankind, to be the chastisers of pride, and the ministers by whom God executes vengeance on atrocious criminals †. This is the consequence of contemplating them as messengers who convey intelligence. They are naturally employed in punishing the crimes whereof they originally gave information.

4. As intelligences who perform so many good offices to the human race, and who are interested so particularly in their concerns, they were proper objects of worship in the judgment of Plato, by whom they are denominated θεους γεννητους και συναρχεντες ‡; and the gifts that are offered to them are said to be acceptable to God §.

* According to the testimony of Florus, Genii were venerated in the most barbarous ages. That historian observes of the Gauls under Brennus, who sacked Rome, that when they entered the Forum, and beheld the aged senators,—ut deos *geniosve* VENERARI cœperunt. De Gest. Roman. lib. i. cap. 13.
† Plut. v. ii. p. 417. ‡ De Legib. l. 13. & Polit.
§ Ibid. l. iv. p. 832. & Epinom. p. 1011.

Thus

(77)

Thus far I have examined the offices of the superior order of Dæmons, who are in general characterized as being the friends of men, and as desirous at all times to promote their best interest *. I do not deny, however, that in the judgment of ancient, as well as of modern writers, who carry the matter much farther than the former, some Genii, even of the higher ranks, are said to bring evils upon mankind from a natural depravity of disposition. Thus Plutarch mentions as the joint opinion of Plato, Xenocrates, and Chryssipus, that there are certain wicked and depraved beings of the dæmoniacal tribes, who delight in giving a bad propensity to human inclinations †: and Pythagoras, according to the testimony of his biographer, was of the same opinion ‡. But some Christian writers having found, (as Origen observes,) that the term Δαιμονων is always taken in an unfavourable sense in the New Testament §, enlarged on every offensive part of the character; while others, overlooking in their de-

---

* Hence the Δαιμονιος has the same signification as felix or divinus, happy or divine, in the writings of Plato. Και ο μεν περι τα τοιαυτα σοφος, δαιμονιος ανηρ. Conviv. p. 1194.

† Oper. v. ii. p. 419.

‡ Laertius numbers diseases as being inflicted on mankind by dæmons, in the opinion of Pythagoras, Υπο τουτω πεμϕισθαι ανθρωποις, τους τε ονειρους, και τα σημεια ΝΟΣΟΥ· Και ν μονον Ανθρωποις, αλλα και προβατοις, &c. l. viii. 587.

§ Cont. Cel. p. 236.

sire

sire to prove that all religious information came originally from the Jews, whatever in these spirits is detrimental or offensive, dwell upon their mediatory employment, as it has already been explained, and find ideal resemblances in the disquisitions of philosophy on this subject to the various offices of Christ*. Accounts of the same things so different, and apparently contradictory, while they afford a cause of triumph to the professed enemies of our religion, serve only to make its friends admit with caution (in the apprehension of injuring the best cause) vague and whimsical applications.

2. From an examination of the department of Genii of primary order, I proceed to consider that which is occupied by those of secondary rank, to whom I apply the epithet terrestrial, as being expressive of their particular appointment. Under this designation I include all those intelligences, who, in consequence of presiding more immediately over the earth, are peculiarly occupied in the care of its inhabitants. I observed formerly that the terrestrial Dæmons are distinguished from the higher order by having bodies of grosser air, suited to the atmosphere wherein they expatiate. I add at present to this observation, that those of this class who have the charge of

* Id. pass.

the

waters, and whom Plato denominates ΗΜΙΘΕΟΙ, become, according to him, slightly visible upon some occasions*. Their appearance, however, at those times was momentary, and calculated to excite, rather than to gratify curiosity. This race of active beings, who are perpetually present with mankind, and are acquainted with their most secret thoughts, possess at the same time the most acute discernment and the most tenacious memory, as faculties that are equally subservient to the purposes of acquiring and of preserving knowledge. Qualified therefore in this manner to give information, they have easy and immediate access to the superior divinities, to whom their communications are at all times acceptable.

Our knowledge of the existence of these Genii, leads us naturally to inquire concerning their subordination, and various employments; questions, that are suggested by their nature and conformity of their motives and disposition to our own. Those whom curiosity may induce to gain information on this subject, will regret that philosophy has not cast greater light on it. We must therefore have recourse to history for examples, whereby the defect of philosophical or traditionary evidence may be in some measure compensated.

* Plat. ubi supra.

In this record of transactions and events, which originating most commonly in the passions of men, determine the character of nations; we mark the traces of four distinct orders, or classes of our busy agents, who, hovering over scenes, of which many are in perpetual fluctuation, influence the thoughts, and direct the actions of mankind. I shall consider each class separately, according to the rank which we suppose it to occupy.

1. It appears then from the testimony of historians, that certain terrestrial Genii of primary importance and dignity, preside over empires, of which they regulate by commission, the various revolutions. Of this kind, is the the genius of Carthage, who is mentioned by Polybius *, that of Fortune, by whom Galba is said to have been accosted †; and the Genius Publicus, as he is denominated, who is said to have appeared upon different occasions to the emperor Julian, announcing his rise and his downfal ‡. The universal belief of this high

* Histor. Lib. xvii.
† Histor. Roman. Script. v. ii. p. 66. Aurel. Allob. 1609.
‡ Ammian Marcellin. apeosd. p. 461 and 501. Videt squalidius (says our author) speciem illam Genii publici, quam cum ad augustum surgeret culmen, conspicit in Gallis; velato cum capite cornu copia per aulæa tristius discedentem.

order

order of Dæmons, that obtained among the Romans, is indicated not only by historians who mention their agency, but by medals that are inscribed to the genius of the empire, or that bear his designation. When therefore we look upon these, as guardian spirits of greater or lesser estimation, according to their different departments, we view them naturally as directing certain events, and conceiving purposes, which, on account of their uniformity and tendency, cannot be attributed to chance. Hence a believer in the doctrine of Genii, was led to regard the many successful efforts of Roman courage and perseverance; as the operation of some tutelary agent of a superior degree, by whom individuals were animated with the hope of victory; and armies conducted at all times, to conquest, and renown. The mind is filled with a great idea, when it contemplates the genius of Carthage, as having contended during three successive wars, with this mighty rival; and having yielded up at last a contest in her favour, by which the fate of the world may be said to have been determined.

2. We may place in the second rank of terrestrial Dæmons, those who in the opinion of the ancients, presided over particular nations; or had the charge of provinces, or cities of distinguished

guished eminence. Temples were raised in different cities to those beings, whose good offices compensated in many instances, the attention that was paid to them; and who gave seasonable warning of impending calamity, short enjoyment or speedy dissolution *. I consider the different appellations of Fortune, and the altars at which she was worshipped †; as monuments erected to Dæmons, or titles bestowed on them, in commemoration of some signal benefit, which it was believed that they had conferred. Athens and Ephesus, under the protection of Minerva and Diana, were indeed patronised by the Diis Majorum Gentium. Cicero takes notice of a beautiful temple at Præneste, that was erected to Fortune under the name SORS; as a tutelary genius ‡: and in fact, this term had the same signification as LAR among ancient writers, both being expressive of local divinities, whose power although circumscribed, was exerted with efficacy in particular departments.

* Some striking examples of this nature are mentioned by the author above quoted. See particularly Hist. Lib. xxiii. ab init.

† Cicero mentions the various designations of Fortune, in enumerating her temples; as the ejus dici of Catulus, after having defeated the Cimbri; Respiciens, Sors, &c.

‡ Oper. p. 530. v. iv.

3. The

3. The third class of the dæmonical tribe, and those in whom man is principally interested, are the peculiar guardians of the human race, to whom the charge of individuals is committed, and who follow them without ceasing through the various stages of their mortal course. As the voice of antiquity, on a point in which human creatures are nearly concerned, must be heard with attention. I shall lay before the reader an account of it, that will tend to gratify curiosity.

The general belief of mankind appears to have been: that a certain order of Genii were appointed by the Supreme Being as guardians of the human race, who, as an inferior species, require protection and defence *. Universal testimony will confer importance in the estimation of a philosopher, upon any tenet, of the truth of which it establishes a favourable prepossession: and this consent must have peculiar efficacy in the present case with Christians, as it confirms a doctrine of revelation †.

---

* Laert. in Prœm. Plut. ubi sup. & de Isid. et Osirid. & Ludov. Viv. Comment. v. i. p. 397.

† This subject is treated at length in a sermon of Dr. James Ogilvie, of Egham, lately published; to which the reader, who may wish to have information on it, is referred.

From Ovid's account of the genealogy of the Lares*, or from other evidences that will afterwards be brought forward: it appears that two beings, of whom one is good, and the other evil, are attendant upon each individual, the former deriving satisfaction from the happiness, and the latter from the misery of his charge. Among those who did not admit the existence of evil Genii; the good or bad success of a man in the general occurrences of life, was conceived to depend in a great degree upon the original strength or weakness of the Spirit or Dæmon, to whom he was given in charge †.

In order to obviate an objection, which will be examined at length in the succeeding section; Plato considers every human Being, as having

---

* The Lares were the two sons of Mercury, by the nymph Lara. Of these, Lar was the good, and Larea the evil genius, who took the charge of infants as soon as they came into the world, and influenced all their future conduct. These Genii were immediate inhabitants of the globe, or of its atmosphere. The belief of their existence is of great antiquity. Diod. Sicul. l. ii. Aug. de Civit. Du. l. x. c. 2.

† According to this doctrine, every man was great or mean, successful or unsuccesful in life, as his genius had ascendency over others, or was subjected by them. Vid. Dodwel Prælect. ii. p. 175.

elected

elected in a pre-existent state, the attendant spirit who is his guardian in the present *. And as the Genii are in his estimation good beings, who delight in performing benevolent offices †; the consequences of having made a proper or an improper choice, which was left to the decision of fortune; affected only comparatively the happiness of the individual; not according to the uprightness or pravity, but in proportion to the power, or impotency of his protector. Hence it happens, that one man, superior perhaps to another in natural abilities, is yet abashed, and daunted in his presence; the Dæmon to whom he is given in charge, being overpowered by that of the latter. Of this nature, was the genius of Cain, compared with that of Abel, according to some writers ‡; and the guardian of Octavius when opposed to that of Antony §. Porphyry ascribes to the same cause, the remarkable superiority of Plotinus, the celebrated Platonic philosopher, to other men; upon whom he looked down with contempt, as beings who shrunk before him into insignificance ||. The wisdom of Socrates **,

* Oper. p. 1054. † Id. p. 537.
‡ Dodwell, ubi supra, August. de Hæres. c. 18.
§ Plut. in Anton. & de Fortun. Roman. Oper. v. ii. p. 319.
|| In Vit. Plotin.
** See particularly the account which Socrates gives of his Dæmon in the Theages of Plato.

the fortune of Cæsar*, and in general the exaltation of mean and often unworthy persons to the highest dignity and dominion †, will be considered as derived from this original by those who believe what history relates concerning the power of the Genii who had them separately in charge ‡.

That this order of beings, so useful to the human race, may be fitted for their peculiar destination, they are said to participate of the imperfections, and even to be actuated in many instances by the passions of mankind §. Entering therefore eagerly into the various and complicated scenes of our enjoyment or distress with superior knowledge and discernment, they are qualified at the same time to heighten our satisfaction in the former state, as much as to alleviate our pain in the latter; although their power extends not in either case to the alteration of events. We may observe, as a confirmation of this remark, that the Dæmon of Socrates was as often unsuccessful in accomplishing the purpose of his warnings, according to the philo-

---

* In his celebrated speech to the mariner, "Thou carriest Cæsar and his *fortune*," he considers the latter as a divinity. Plut. in Cæsar.

† Vitellius, Nero, Caligula, &c.

‡ Apul. ap. August. de Civit. Dei, l. viii. c. 16.

§ Apul. ap. Aug. de Civit. Dei, l. viii. c. 16.

sopher's

sopher's own account of the matter, as the contrary. This tutelary being obtained indeed his end with Socrates himself. But the decisions of destiny, under the direction of the Δημιουργος, were not levelled to the comprehension of either party; far less were these subjected to their control. The former announced events which he was unable to prevent, and the latter gave warning of dangers that were neither averted nor postponed *.

As far as we have yet gone our observations have respected those of the present rank of Genii, who delight in the performance of good offices. But I have already evinced, that of this order the members are not universally upright, even in the judgment of ancient as well as modern writers †; and according to both, the calamities of life, and particularly the sufferings of good men, point as immediately to the hand of a bad, as more favourable circumstances to the agency of a good spirit. Final events (as I have already observed) are out of the question. I mean only to trace the slight step of superior agents on the chequered path of human life, and to render manifest the con-

* As in the cases of Charmides, Timarchus, Throsyllus, &c. Plat. ubi sup.
† Plut. v. ii. p. 419. and in Brut. v. i.

cern which they appear to take in its transactions.

Among the various phænomena which philosophy has in all ages attempted to illustrate, that of dreaming has perhaps occasioned as much speculation as any other *; the visions of the night, which at some times are the reveries of a sportful imagination, having exhibited upon many interesting occasions, prophetic images of events slumbering on the bosom of futurity. Of representations thus diversified, some of which the purpose was obviously beneficial, indicated the care of a benevolent and watchful guardian; as others of an opposite tendency, discovered the busy operation of a malevolent spirit, obtruding upon the thought scenes of misery, whereof the effect was heightened by anticipation and suspence. Of the former kind, was the dream of Socrates recorded in Crito, and that

* Aristotle observes in his history of animals, that there have been instances of men and women who were never known to dream. To some of these, he says, the first deviation from their usual insensibility have been followed either by death or sickness. Our great philosopher relates this fact without accounting for it. The intelligent reader will however judge, that the evils which, in the present case, were consequent on dreaming, arose from the change of temperament that produced this phænomenon. Oper. v. i. p. 831.

of Eudamas, mentioned by Cicero, as well as many others of the same nature, which it is unnecessary to enumerate. Of the latter denomination, are those dark presages of future events, ascribed in some instances to the agency of evil Dæmons; that have at times produced the worst effects on a gloomy and distempered imagination *.

Now if we acknowledge, that favourable presages of future events, have been suggested on some occasion by good Genii; we may admit also that those of a contrary nature, and tendency, derive their origin from beings of opposite disposition. I therefore infer with equal reason, that there are bad spirits, by whose operation, on the organs of sense, detrimental consequences have been produced; as the effects of a nature altogether different, indicate the existence and agency of those that have benevolence: and in this judgment we are supported by the authority of the ancients †.

* Aug. de Civit. Dei, v. i. p. 718.
† That dreams were held in reverence by the sages of antiquity as presages of future events, will be obvious, when we reflect that Plato considers dreaming as a species of divination, of which we have seen that Dæmons are acknowledged to be authors. An ονειροκριτης, or an interpreter of dreams was appointed, according to our author, as certainly as a Pythia in the temple of Apollo, to receive the oracular afflatus.

From

From the probable conjecture of philosophy concerning the existence of evil Genii, when we apply to history for positive evidence; the story of Brutus is immediately recollected as a fact that establishes this doctrine *. The proof whereby the appearance of the evil genius of the illustrious Roman is supported, makes the whole account as credible, as any account can be made by the concurrence of circumstances in a case of this kind. And he, who believes that Brutus, who was strictly virtuous, had such an attendant; will surely find no difficulty in giving faith, either to any similar narration, or to the general position which it is proposed to concern.

4. I shall dismiss this branch of the present subject, when I have observed, that we may consider as a fourth class of terrestrial Genii, inferior in rank to the former; the Dryads, Hamadryades, Satyrs, Wood-nymphs †, and in

---

* Plut. in Brut. Flor. l. iv. c. 7. Appian. l. iv.

† These were known by the various appellations of Oreades, Nereides, Naiades, from the fields, fountains, and rivers, over which they presided. Of the whole tribes, the Hamadryads, (whose duration was coeval with that of the tree which they inhabited ;) were the shortest lived, as well as most dependent on the compassion of mankind. Some pathetic tales have been founded on this circumstance. See Ovid's

in general, the whole race of beings who have the charge of rivers, forests, fields and fountains; the subjects of many beautiful poetical fables.

Upon the whole therefore we may venture to pronounce, that a review of the scenes which the philosophers of ancient Greece have presented as the theme of the preceding remarks, afford a lively representation of the character of its inhabitants. The busy ingenuity of this happy race imparted life to all obejcts indiscriminately; nature teemed around them with universal animation; the fields, the groves, the fountains, the forests, the very air of this delightful region, were prolific, and the face of the country displaying alternately, villas and statues, lawns and altars; the harvests of Ceres, the shades, of Diana, the haunts of the Naiads, and the gardens of Pomona, presented testimonies in every quarter of genius, elegance, and supersti-

---

Ovid's Metam. l. viii. v. 749, &c. Homer Hymn. in Vener. Apollon. Rhad. l. ii. v. 480. The combat of the river, God Xanthus with Achilles, forms an interesting scene of the Iliad. And in general, the interview of an hero with a goddess; or of a Wood-nymph, or Hamadryad with an accidental traveller, furnished a suitable birth to some prince, who was destined to figure in the fabulous ages, and introduced him with dignity on the stage.

tious

tious observance. The Athenians, wasting their hours in the pursuit of novelty, cease when thus contemplated to be regarded with wonder; and the altar inscribed to the ιγνωτο Θεω, among so many other religious monuments, becomes familiar as a characteristical indication.

SECT.

SECTION IV.

CREATION AND CONSTITUENT PRINCIPLES OF MAN.

HAVING now examined at considerable length the nature of the Being who framed, and the invisible inhabitants, who people the universe, according to the theory of Plato, as well as of other ancient philosophers, I come to a branch of my subject wherein human beings are more immediately interested; I mean the creation and constituent principles of MAN. I shall follow in treating of this doctrine, the order which I observed formerly, by laying before the reader the tenets and maxims of other philosophers on these heads, as being introductory to those of Plato; which they tend also to enforce and illustrate.

Man, according to the Magi, who were followers of Zoroaster, is principally constituted of an intelligent and immortal spirit, which descended from heaven, in order to communicate its influence during a certain appointed season to the body, wherein it is the cause or principle of animation. Of regions that are occupied by spirits in their state of pre-existence, they believed

(94)

lieved that some are splendid and luminous, others involved in impenetrable night, and that a third participated of both qualities. The spirit by whom man is animated, descends originally from the enlightened region, to which, (if it should merit the reward by adequate service;) it is permitted at the instant of its separation from the body to return. Otherwise it is received according to the degree of its demerit into the middle region, or is cast into that of darkness*. On this account, no precept was enforced with greater energy by those teachers of wisdom, than that which enjoins watchfulness against contamination arising from the union of mind with body. They represented the latter, which is gross, mortal, and corruptible, as an incumbrance to the operation of the pure spirit; and the indulgence of its appetites, as terminating in final destruction: figured in the high eastern stile, by a translation to the horrible abode of necessity †.

Although the body of man, consisting of impurities collected from the four elements, is itself of no estimation, yet when it is considered as the habitation of an intelligent spirit, (which

* Plethon. Expos. Oracul. Magicor. p. 81.
† Εκπιπτων—ὑφ' ην εις δεινην τινα και απαρατρεπτην αναγκην. Id. p. 82.

those

those philosophers denominated a spark of fire emitted from the Deity*;) we should err in neglecting to pay proper attention to it: for the purpose of its divine inhabitant is to purify it gradually from every pollution, and to ascend in it at last, as in a fiery vehicle, to the place from which it came. In this account of the animal nature of man, refined and purified by the spirit, with which it mounts to the higher regions, it will appear afterwards, that the Chaldeans differ from the Greeks who considered the former as mortal. I mention this tenet, however, as containing a sublime, and perhaps an appropriated idea of the nature and influence of pure spirit upon the mansion which it has occupied. It brings before the mind the picturesque description of the ascent of Elijah by the inspired historian—" Behold, there appeared a chariot of fire, and horses of fire. And Elijah went up by a whirl-wind into heaven †."

We have already seen that Anaxagoras was the first of ancient philosophers, (according to the testimony of some writers;) who introduced mind into the universe. In his system, animals

---

* Μοιρης δε της θειας τρεπεται το πραγμα χαριτος, της τω απορρητω πυρι τη υλην εκ δαπανωσης τε σωματος, και την εμφυτον και γεωδη ζωην οχηματι πυρινω μετεωριζουσης.

† 2 Kings, chap. ii. v. 11.

were

were produced by the combination of humidity, heat, and earth, or matter, coalescing into different forms, and constituting after this manner the various species of creatures, who afterwards generated each other *. A Mind, or Supreme Architect, over-ruled in his theory the whole procedure; and after having communicated these qualities to the elements, superintended the production of beings endowed with life, whom he adapted to their different spheres of operation. The intelligent reader will perceive, that this scheme is founded upon that of Thales, which has been explained at some length. It contains, however, a considerable improvement of the hypothesis of that philosopher, and presents to imagination the *spirit*, who in the sublime language of the Bard of Paradise,

> Dove-like sat brooding on the vast abyss,
> And made it pregnant.

It ought to be remarked, that this philosopher who accounts, as we have seen, for the origin of body, is said to have entertained a very false and inadequate idea of the human soul, which he confounded with the animal, or sensitive spirit †. His scheme therefore in this point appears to have been essentially defective.

As

---

* Laert. Anaxag. l. ii.
† Aristotle animadverts, with great justice and propriety,
on

As Anaxagoras, in the preceding passage, seems to have improved the system of Thales, a sect of oriental philosophers, whose principles are recorded by Maimonides, have made a similar amendment on that of Epicurus. The atoms, of which the fortuitous concourse framed the universe in the judgment of the latter, in that of the former were created and animated by the Supreme Being. Each particle also of those which compose the human form, has existence according to their opinion. They maintain different notions concerning the nature of the soul, and its place of residence. Some taught, that of the many atoms by whose coalition the human body is constituted, the spirit informs some single particle or substance: and that the whole mass is said to be animated, in consequence of the existence that is imparted to that portion of it. Others, on the contrary, believed, that the

---

on this error of Anaxagoras. Πολλακις το αιτιον τη καλως και ορθως τον ΝΟΥΝ λεγει· ετιρωθι δε, τον Νουν ειναι τον αυτον τη Ψυχη, εν απασι γαρ υπαρχει εν τοις ζωοις, και μεγαλοις, και μικροις, &c. The remark of our acute critic on this doctrine is, that the soul considered as comprehending intellect, far from being in all animals, is not even in all men. Ου φαινεται δε ο γε κατα Φρενησιν λεγομενος Νους πασιν ομοιως υπαρχειν τοις ζωοις, αλλ᾽ ουδε τοις Ανθρωποις πασιν. Oper. v. i. p. 619. Perhaps the reader will judge that the last words of this sentence are written in the character of a satyrist, and are rather witty than philosophically true.

soul consists of many subtle intermixtures, possessing some accident whereby existence is communicated to these, and is consubstantiated with the body *.

We may observe in general concerning these, and other theories on the same subject that might be enumerated, that while their authors consider the mind as a substance distinct from the body, wherewith it is said to be united, they fail in distinguishing its powers of perception, reason, intelligence, &c. as indicating *a divine original*, from the passions and grosser appetites which arise from its union with matter. The reader will not receive much information in knowing, that Aristotle gave to the mind, which he defined to be a fifth nature or element, distinct from all others, the appellation Εντελεχεια, as expressive of its perfection, or, according to Cicero, of its immense activity †; that by Zeno, it was termed fire ‡, that its seat was by some philosophers supposed to be the heart §, by others the brain; and in investigating hypotheses of similar import. Without therefore enlarging farther on this branch of my subject,

* De More Nevoch. c. lxxiii. p. 152, &c.
† Arist. de Anima, l. i. c. 2. Laert. l. v. p. 322. Cicer. Oper. v. iv. p. 355.
‡ Id. ibid.   § Id. ibid.

I pro-

I proceed to explain the doctrine of Pythagoras on the present point, as being immediately introductory to that of Plato.

The soul of man, according to the Pythagorean notions, consists of four principles, or faculties: mind, science or intelligence, opinion, sense. In one or other of those intellectual powers, all arts and sciences have their original. The mind is a monad, or is essentially one, as we may perceive by all its operations. This truth will be obvious, if we reflect that whatever the mind discerns, it discerns as having unity. Thus sense is employed in taking cognisance of a multitude of men, of whom we cannot compute the number. But the mind forms, in contemplating this multitude, the simple idea of *man*, to which nothing is similar. Judging in the same manner concerning all other animals, it discovers the radical quality, or character, whereby the kind is distinguished, and defines the species by that predominant disposition. Thus man is a *reasoning*, a horse, a neighing animal, &c. We denominate therefore that intelligent principle one, with strict propriety, which perceives at all times unity in the objects of which it judges of the properties, or investigates the nature *.

* The original, which is too long to be inserted here, is in Plutarch De Placit. Philos. Oper. v. ii. p. 876.

It ought farther to be remarked, that we are made sensible by reflection, that man possesses, with the faculty of reason, whereby he is distinguished from all other animals; sense and passions, which he shares in common with them. Intellect is characteristical of man properly so called. It is not less discriminated from the passions and grosser appetites by its place of residence, than by its operations. While those have their seat in the heart, which they agitate at pleasure, this ruling faculty occupies the head, or superior part of the body, wherein it controles and regulates the subordinate members. Finally, while those corporeal qualities which man possesses in common with other animals, are extinguished at death; this emanation of the Deity, by which he is essentially constituted, is invisible and immortal *. The veins, nerves, and arteries of the body, may be denominated the chains which retain this inhabitant during a season in captivity †. But, at the instant when these are broken, it reascends to the element of air, wherein it expatiates at freedom; retaining the human form which it formerly possessed ‡.

* το μεν φρονιμον αθανατον· τα δε λοιπα θνητα.

† Δεσμα δε ειναι της Ψυχης, τας φλεβας και τας αρτεριας, και τα νευρα οταν δε ισχυη, και καθαυτην γενομενη ηρεμη, δεσμα γενεσθαι αυτης τους λογους, και τα εργα.

‡ Εκχυθεισαν δε αυτην επι γης, υπαζεσθαι εν τω αερι, ομοιαν τω σωματι. Laert. Lib. viii. p. 586.

These

These outlines of the Pythagorean doctrine, concerning the formation and constituent principles of man, naturally introduce the Platonic account of this important subject, the various parts of which come now successively to be reviewed.

Man is compounded, according to Plato, of three parts; the ΝΟΥΣ or mind, the intelligent spirit, the sensitive soul or Ψυχη, and the Σωμα or body the receptacle of both. This division (which is evidently that of the apostle St. Paul, 1 Thessal. v. 23.) is founded in observations on human nature, of which reflection will enable us to comprehend the truth and propriety.

When we consider that microcosm, (as Plato calls it,) the human mind, and attempt to analize its various qualities, operations that originate in this diversity are presented to us, which are not without difficulty reconciled. A view of this nature will serve to convince a rational inquirer, that reason and the passions are so opposite to each other, the tendency of the latter being at all times that of obstructing the influence of the former, that philosophers were naturally led to consider each as having a distinct original. They observed in following out this idea, that the intellect acting at liberty, and regulating the motions of subordinate propensities, is no improper image of the Supreme Mind, animating the parts and directing the government of the universe: those sensibilities, on the other hand, whereby the animal spirits are disturbed and agitated, they judged to be inseparably connected with corporeal substance, wherewith it hath the same original and dissolution. Hence arose the celebrated distinction, so familiar to ancient philosophers, of a rational and sensitive soul. A particular account of the former is at this time unnecessary, as I shall treat of it at large in the succeeding sections. A few general remarks it is however proper to introduce.

The intelligent spirit of man is not derived, according to our author, from the parent, but pre-existed in its animation of a corporeal form in a state of happiness with beings of superior order*. This spirit participates of the nature of God †, to whom it returns at the instant of its separation from the body ‡, unless it be polluted with crimes which render its purification indispensibly necessary. In this case, it either passes into different forms according to the na-

* P. 1008, 1073, and Phed. pass.

† Συγγενης τω Θεω και αθανατω και αει οντι. De Repub. lib. x. and p. 837.   ‡ P. 1148.

ture

ture and tendency of its actions *, or suffers through *all time* the punishment of atrocious wickedness, terminating in final impenitence, in a place prepared for that purpose †. Finally, this spirit is always distinguished by Plato, as we have seen that it was by Pythagoras, from the animal or sensitive principle, as being nobler and more excellent ‡. It is with this purpose sometimes termed Θειον, divine, by the former, and sometimes Ηγουμενον, the ruling or governing spirit, in order to denote its power and efficacy §.

As the rational soul is thus the seat of understanding, so the animal or sensitive part of man contains those irregular desires and that concupiscence which we share in common with inferior creatures ‖. This being, denominated το θνητον or mortal, is compounded of elementary sub-

---

* P. 1054, 765, 1223, &c.

† The words of Plato are πασχοντας τον αει χρονον, p. 358. The periphrasis whereby the duration of punishment is here described, does not immediately imply eternity, to signify which he would have used the term αιδιονην, or αιωνον. In the text therefore, I adopt the same, that, in my opinion, most obvious, as being that of our author, although I differ from his commentators, and particularly from Dacier in this matter.

‡ Plut. v. ii. p. 943. Cier. and Laert. ubi supra Aristot. de Anim. lib. i. c. 2.

§ Plat. p. 1054. ‖ Laert. Plat. p. 240.

stances, but has neither the same original, dignity, character, or duration, as that which is an image of the Creator. Upon the whole, therefore, it is considered as the vehicle or medium whereby spirit is united to grosser matter. In this respect also the sensitive soul of man has the advantage of mere animal nature, that its coalescence with intellect in the human species renders those actions properly virtuous which in brutes result from instinctive propensity, without knowledge of circumstance, or apprehension of danger. Thus the same impulse of propensity, which in a lion, or a bear, is termed brutal ferocity; takes in a man, the nobler designation of intrepidity or fortitude; in consequnce of that sagacity, whereby, as a rational agent, it is supposed that his actions are directed.

Thus distinguished in its nature from the purer intelligence, the animal part of man is not less distinct from the former, in its original. An account of the doctrine of Plato on this subject, will lead us into an examination of the boldest and most ingenious of all his theological tenets.

Among other new theories that are opened in the Timæus, one particularly respects the creation

creation of Deities, who are said to be of an inferior order, though they were worshipped by heathen nations as having Supreme authority, and dominion. These are Jupiter, Juno, Rhæa, and the whole tribe of Pagan divinities, who received existence, according to our author, from one Supreme Mind, for certain purposes which he enumerates; of these, one of the principal is, their partial interference in the creation of man.

The TO EN, the great Creator, after having called into existence the beings above mentioned, acquaints them of his purpose to make a creature, who would be rendered immortal by the practice of virtue, and might be termed divine. He observes, that if all the powers which would meet in this production, should come from himself, those who possessed them would be equal with the Gods. "To you therefore, he says, (addressing the inferior Deities,) I consign the part of adding a mortal to the immortal spirit which will proceed from myself."—Having thus spoken, he proceeded to create the inhabitants of the stars, and planetary orbs, of the same substance and materials as had been used in constituting the Anima Mundi. These, after having occupied the material forms prepared for their reception by the younger offspring of heaven,

ven, were dismissed to different places of residence. The human race consists of two sexes, of the principal of which, the term man in its most limited acceptation, is characteristical. This workmanship of omnipotence, has, according to our author, two souls, or intelligent principles. Of these, one proceeding immediately from the first mover, is pure as his own essence, and is framed as the celestial Beings, for immortality. Into the latter, which is mortal, the passions enter, and appetites that are inimical to happiness.

Having gone thus far, God willed that the rational and sensitive spirit, so different from each other in their nature should be placed apart. He therefore constituted the head to be the seat of intellect, where the divine inhabitant remains uncontaminated by its communication with sordid appetites. The animal substance, the work of subordinate Deities, was placed by them in the breast and heart, the seat of the passions and desires. The operation of spirits thus distinct, exerted in complicated senses, and exciting alternate contempt, and admiration, constitutes all that variety of character occasioned by the collision of opposite and independant qualities, which we include under the simple, but comprehensive epithet—MAN.

I have

I have thus endeavoured to lay before the reader, the principal of those many hypotheses, whereby the wisdom of the ancients attempted to account for phenomena, of the nature and cause of which the mind is at all times solicitous to receive information. Every intelligent reader will, no doubt, be ready to remark, the relation which the scheme of Plato in the latter instance bears to that of Pythagoras. Resemblances of a similar nature will be found in all the branches of our author's theology. The tenets however of the Samian sage, improved and embellished, by the splendid imagination of his illustrious successor, are seen to the greatest advantage by the dress wherein they are clothed, and by the principles with which they are united; and the consonancy of those eminent philosophers in their ideas, will at all times establish a prepossession in favour of the *truth* of doctrines that are at the same time consistent with those of revelation.

To the reader, who after having followed our author through so many intricate disquisitions, may find relief in contemplating even a feeble imitation of his manner, I would observe, that a view of the Platonic universe, peopled with innumerable inhabitants, suggests the idea of an hive, occupied by a busy community, and replete

plete with a treasure collected from all quarters. In this comparison, if we consider the exterior frame of the cell surrounding and protecting the insect tribes, as an image of that immense circumference whereby the globe is invested, the ideas that *live* in the Divine Mind, and pour in uninterrupted succession in all parts of its workmanship will, be figured by the swarm, that bursting from multiplied compartments, settle promiscuously on objects, of which they extract the essence, and exhibit the patterns: the queen of these tribes, the soul as she may be termed of the whole body, whose influence extends to all parts of her dominion, is no inadequate emblem of the vital spirit, the Anima Mundi, who fills and agitates the frame of the world: in fine, the honey dropping on all sides into the combs wherewith the hive is replenished, represents not improperly in this group of resemblances, the instructive nature of the Platonic philosophy, and the sweetness of those periods wherein its maxims are conveyed.

SECTION V.

THEORIES OF THE ANCIENTS, AND PARTICU-
LARLY OF PLATO, CONCERNING THE ORI-
GIN OF EVIL, AND ITS EFFECTS.

FROM the various prospects of the world, and its inhabitants, that have been offered to observation in the preceding pages, our attention is now called in following out the present subject, to points, in the contemplation of which rational beings have exercised at all times the powers of understanding. Of these, complex and multiplied as they are, we may venture to affirm, that no doctrine whatever has been more universally investigated by men of speculation, than that of which I propose to treat in this section; a circumstance, which the nature of the subject will prevent us from considering as extraordinary.

Admiration of the great Author of Nature, and an high sense of his perfections, were succeeded in the minds of the first men by inquiries that related immediately to their own particular circumstances and situation. As soon as their thoughts were turned into this channel from their original objects, they felt that emotions excited in the heart by love and reverence of the Supreme Mind, were checked almost as soon as they arose, by the reflection that evil had crept by some strange and unaccountable accident into the grand and masterly fabric of the universe, and by having marked the ruin and devastation that are attendant on her progress. A consequence arising naturally from the consideration of these defects was, that men of discernment began to speculate concerning the causes for which they were permitted to take place, and to inquire whether this phænomenon in the workmanship of the Deity could be accounted for without being led to him as its original. Hence it happened that a question, which the sages of the first as well as of later ages, have been employed at all times in resolving to satisfaction, is that which relates to the origin of evil.

Of the various hypotheses whereby men who were unacquainted with the doctrines of revelation, have endeavoured to solve the difficulties of this inquiry, the three following appear to me as those that principally merit attention. These are, the scheme of Zoroaster, the celebrated author of the good and evil principle; that of Chrysippus, who inculcated the doctrine of fate or necessity; and the theory of our author, which, as I shall afterwards endeavour to evince,

is

is different from both. The remarks of other philosophers, who delight in cavilling at the present dispensation of things without attempting to vindicate its author, will naturally fall into our examination.

1. The first view of this subject carries our eyes towards the east, where we see Zoroaster instructing the Persians at a very early period of society*, in the knowledge of Zedydan and Ahriman, or according to the Greek pronuncia-

* It is not my present business to ascertain the time at which Zoroaster, or Zerdust, the legislator and teacher of oriental nations, promulgated his doctrines. There would indeed be some difficulty in accomplishing this purpose, as authors differ widely from each other in their accounts of Zoroaster. Thus, while according to one historian, he was contemporary with Ninus, king of Assyria; he is said by another to have lived under Darius Hystaspes: and in the same spirit, five hundred and five thousand years, before the Trojan war, have been assigned as the period at which he flourished. Justin. lib. i. Ammian. Marcellin. lib. xxiii. Plin. lib. xxx. cap. 1. Plutarch. de Isid. and Osiris. I know no method of reconciling these relations, unless we believe that they refer to different persons. All authors however agree in ascribing the invention of magic to a man who bore the name of Zoroaster, whom they also consider as the first author of that scheme of the origin of evil, which, under the appellation of the manichean hypothesis, has been explained and supported, as containing the only rational account of this phœnomenon.

tion, of Oromages and Arimanius, the two great causes of good and evil. Our oriental philosopher taught, in that stile of personification, which was most acceptable to his countrymen; that Oromages, who was himself the offspring of the purest light, created six inferior deities, who were distinguished by the characters of benevolence, truth, equity, wisdom, &c. as beings who participated of his nature, and would render his influence universal*. He ascended afterwards into the superior regions. peopled the heavens with constellations, and inclosed (says our author in a beautiful stile of imagery) many other divinities in an egg, which was afterwards broken and contaminated by the evil offspring of Arimanius.

This malignant principle, the natural enemy of the source of rectitude and benevolence, employed that creative energy which he also possessed in the production of intelligences who were hostile to Oromages and his followers. Arimanius sprung originally from darkness. He and his offspring, having broken the egg of Oromages, mixed among those purer spirits who were placed in it, and spreading with them in common over the world, obstructed at all times and marred their operations. Hence, good and evil, right and

* Plutarch, de Isid. and Osirid.

wrong,

wrong, appear to be blended promiscuously in the constitution and government of the universe. A period however will come, at which Arimanius and his followers will be finally exterminated; when the earth also, divested of the mountains that roughen its surface, will be the habitation of happy men, the members of one great community, speaking the same language, and animated by the same vital and universal principle. *.

Between those powers, who are perpetually at variance, Zoroaster placed a mediatory being, named Mithra, and by the Persians, Mesites, who appears to have executed the same office as the goddess Αρμονια of the Chaldeans, and somewhat similar to that of Hermes, the Διακτορος, or intermediate messenger of the Greeks †.

Such are the outlines of that celebrated doctrine, wherein modern philosophers of great eminence have pretended to find the only rational account of the origin of evil.

When we consider the scheme of a good and evil principle, apart from the fabulous circum-

* Plutarch, vol. ii. p. 370. As a confirmation that this was the doctrine of Zoroaster, we may observe that it corresponds to the strain of an Arabian author, whose account is quoted at large by Dr. Hyde in his work De Religion. Vet. Persar. c. 22.

† Iliad, lib. xxiv.

stances that embellish the narration, its antiquity, as having originated among a simple race of men at an early period of society, establishes a favourable prepossession of its truth, as being congenial (if we may thus express it) to the mind, and suggested spontaneously by the first view of the subject. A minute examination of this well-known hypothesis would lead me from the professed purpose of this essay, which is to explain the theories of ancient theologians, without investigating at all times their nature or opposing their evidence. I observe therefore only at present, that men in general, and particularly that good men, will find an insuperable objection to the theory of Zoroaster and his followers, in the difficulty, if not impossibility, of conceiving an idea of a being of perfect pravity, whose pleasure arises solely from the production of evil, and whose highest enjoyment lies in the contemplation of misery. I consider as one of the best proofs, that there is a principle of benevolence and rectitude in man, and that the good tendencies of his nature surpass their contraries; that although his mind readily admits the idea of perfect excellence, it is invincibly repugnant to its opposite. Some latent spark of commiseration, some native propensity that is allied to virtue, are ingredients of every character whereof he exhibits a representation, or even forms a conception.

Hence

Hence Arimanius, as a malevolent being, in whom evil dispositions at all times predominate, and are exerted to the injury of mankind, may be supposed to have existence, while as an intelligence, whose thoughts are wholly occupied in effecting mischief, and in whose mind order and harmony are alone the objects that produce disquietude, we may venture to affirm, that he had no fixed establishment even in the opinion of philosophers who hold him up to observation *.

But to whatever objections this doctrine may justly give occasion, we may yet say with truth that it was originally framed with the purpose of

* Some readers will find a striking evidence of the truth of this remark in the SATAN of Milton, as it is displayed in various points of view to our observance in his divine poem. Our great poet was sensible, that in order to interest his readers in the fate and actions of this personage it was necessary that the native malignity and pravity of the *Author of Evil* should be chequered with qualities that excite admiration. Hence, even in attempting to accomplish the ruin of mankind, unshaken fortitude, invincible courage, adherence to his ultimate purpose in circumstances the most hopeless and desperate, and even pity for the innocence which he is about to violate, are thrown with exquisite discernment into his character. In this various and interesting assemblage we find that attention is kept constantly awake, and that passions are involuntarily and powerfully excited, which, in the contemplation of a being *purely evil*, would have yielded to apathy or been absorbed in detestation.

vin-

vindicating God from the charge of being the author of sin. In this respect, the plan of our oriental philosopher has the advantage of that of Epicurus, who states in very clear and forcible terms, the argument against the moral perfections of the Deity arising from the introduction of evil, as his words are quoted by Lactantius*. Instead of attempting to substitute a better scheme in place of that which he endeavours to subvert, this philosopher leaves us no other resource, than that of denying the superintendency of Providence over a world, in the government of which, neither wisdom nor justice are conspicuous. All these ends are accomplished with great facility by Epicurus, who seems to have been endowed for this purpose with an eye that wandered over the universe, without marking the traces of design in its formation, and with appetites to which he accommodated his divinities, that they might not obtrude reflection upon his hours of enjoyment, or overshadow his prospects by unwelcome anticipation.

The doctrine of the Chaldeans on this subject, as it is laid down by Plutarch, is evidently founded upon that of Zoroaster. They believed, that of the planets, whom they denomi-

* Lactan. De Ira Dei.

nated

nated Gods, two were employed in good offices, two in evil occupations, and that three were of a middle order, participating of the nature of both. To the same source we may trace the received opinion of the Greeks, who ascribed, as our author observes, the good that takes place in the world to Olympian Jupiter, and the evil to infernal * Pluto. These correspond to Oromages and Arimanius, in the same manner as we have already seen, that the goddess Αρμονια, Harmony, coincides with Mithra, the intermediate divinity of our oriental philosopher, whom she resembles also in her office and department. This being was said to have sprung from Mars and Venus; of whom the former is cruel and contentious, the latter mild and genial. By partaking therefore of the qualities of both, she was peculiarly fitted for the middle station which she was said to have occupied.

2. Hitherto, however inadequate the scheme which we have mentioned may be to its ultimate purpose, we cannot accuse the philosophers who support it, of maintaining dogmas that are inconsistent and contradictory. The doctrine of

* The Greek term is αποροπαιφ Αδου, a term that is applied to express the difficulty of egress from the dominions of Pluto, and cannot be translated as an epithet applied to the God.

a good and an evil principle is an uniform tenet, of which the nature and tendency may be understood without difficulty. But, with the opinion of stoical philosophers on this subject, the matter is greatly different. Their notions of the origin of evil are, at the same time, so inconclusive and undetermined, so various and incongruous with each other, that the celebrity of the founders is the principal cause for which we bring their tenets into one point of view, as without these many readers might think that we had not done justice to the subject. That I may not therefore omit any theory on this head, that is or may be judged to be material, I lay down the following propositions, as comprehending whatever authors of this tribe have advanced on this interesting doctrine.

1. These philosophers agree in acknowledging, that one Supreme Being (to whom however they apply different designations,) presides in the universe, whereof every part is animated by his influence*.

> Deum namque ire per omnes
> Terrasque tractusque maris, cœlumque profundum
> Hinc pecudes, armenta, viros, genus omne ferarum,
> Quemque sibi tenues nascentem arcessere vitam.
> Virgil.

* Ἐν το εἶναι θεον και Νουν, και εἱμαρμενην, και Δια, πολλακις τε παυμαις ὀνομασι αἱς προσονομα ζεσθαι. Posidon. ap. Deogon. Laert. Zenon. Lib. vii. p. 520.

2. To

2. To this Being they gave the appellation fate, destiny, necessity, in order to evince the truth of their great tenet, that all things whatever originate in him, upon whom they have fixed an unalterable dependence. Thus Chrysippus, according to Cicero, denominated God the necessity of future events *; and Seneca applies to him the term fate, as being expressive of the great cause or principle to which all events are suspended †. *Fate*, in the judgment of the former philosopher, is the epithet whereby we express an eternal succession and revolution of things involving each other in an uninterrupted series ‡. To this series it is that the poets allude in mentioning the *Parcæ* or destinies, the daughters, as Plato calls them, of necessity §, whom they sometimes confound with that fate of whom they are said to be the ministers.

3. From this account of the first cause, it follows, that the evil which we observe to take place

* Chrysippus Deum dicit esse—fatalem umbram, & necessitatem rerum futurarum. De Natur. Deor. Lib. i. cap. 15.

† Vis illum FATUM vocare? Non errabis. *Hic* est ex quo suspensi sunt omnia. Natur. Quest. Lib. ii. cap. 45.

‡ Fatum inquit Chrysippus, est sempiterna quædam & indeclinabilis series rerum et catena, volvens semetipsa sese, et implicans per æternos consequentiæ ordines, ex quibus apta connexaque est. Aul. Gell. Lib. vi. cap. 2.

§ De Repub. Lib. x.

in the world, must be traced up to him as its original; otherwise, with what propriety can it be said, that all things are suspended under him as the links of a chain that terminates at the hand by which it was framed, and is supported *? It is idle to distinguish with stoical philosophers, between causes that are perfect and principal, and those that are assisting and approximate in the production of this effect; or to say that the laws of necessity operate upon the mind according to its qualities and information †: for the decree whereby the actions of an individual are necessarily regulated, must extend to the whole species. He therefore who affirms that any distinction is made by the Author of Nature between a well and an ill-informed understanding, charges him with weakness and injustice; weakness, in

* This consequence of the scheme of Chrysippus is urged with great force by the author above quoted. Si Chrysippus Fato putat omnia monere, et regi, nec declinari transcendique posse agmina Fati, & volumina; peccata quoque hominum et delicta, non sustentanda neque condicenda sunt ipsis voluntatibus eorum; sed Necessitati cuidam, et instantiæ quæ oritura FATO—per quam necesse sit fieri quicquid futurum est. Aul. Gell. ubi supra.

† Quanquam ita sit, inquit Chrysippus, ut ratione quadam principali necessario coacta atque connexa sunt omnia fato, ingenia tamen ipsa mentium nostrarum proinde sunt fato obnoxia, ut proprietas eorum est ipsa, et qualitas: nam si sint per naturam salubriter utiliterque ficta, omnem illam vim quæ de fato extrinsecus ingruit inoffensius tractabiliusque transmittunt, &c. Ibid.

per-

permitting that his decrees should be influenced at any time by the purpose to which qualities may be applied that were conferred originally by himself; and injustice, in making a distinction that is founded in partiality, and is subversive of the rights of mankind.

4. Good and evil, justice and injustice, were, in the opinion of the Stoics, and indeed, as we shall see afterwards, in the judgment of Plato himself, self-existent and essential principles, of which neither can subsist without its opposite. Evil therefore was, in their estimation, thus far subservient to the purpose of utility, that the good which is blended with it in the universe, may be said to exist in its contrary, whereof the union is upon the whole beneficial *. Our ideas of both, therefore, are always associated: and as the thought of good excites at all times some conception of the evil that is opposed to it, the latter exists as indispensibly and immediately as the former †. The absurdity of this doctrine is exposed with much strength and propriety by Plutarch, who observes, that according to it we must believe, that at the period when God will

---

* Η δε κακια προς τα λειπα συμπτωματα εχει χορον. Γιγνητε γαρ αυτη κατα το της φυσεως λογον· Και ινος ουτως ειπω εκ αχρηστως γινεται προς τα ολα· ουδε γαρ τ'Αγαθον ην. Plutarch. Oper. Vol. ii. p. 1065.

† Thæctet. p. 129.

reunite

reunite all things in himself, and will finally expel whatever is pernicious from the universe; there will be no good in it, because there cannot any longer be evil. He farther remarks, that according to the same principle, we ought to pray for the continuance of fraud, lying, hypocrisy, and other similar vices in the world; because as soon as these cease to operate in society, the opposite virtues must also be exterminated *.

I cannot dismiss this subject without observing, that the followers of Chrysippus would have found their account much more effectually in maintaining, that the evils of life have their use in calling forth the manly virtues, resignation, and fortitude into exercise, virtues that command the admiration of mankind, than in endeavouring to establish the absurd and unintelligible maxim above mentioned, of which our author has well explained the consequences. The ills, as they are termed, that take place in the world, answer the same purpose when considered in this point of view, as bitter or acid ingredients mixed in a medicinal draught with more palatable materials, by improving at the same time its qualities, and by rendering its efficacy complete.

* Plut. ubi sup.

5. Although.

5. Although we have seen that the Stoics made use of a prosopopœia in denoting the Supreme Being by the term fate, or necessity; it is yet certain that they considered Jupiter, the father of the universe, as the only perfect and incorruptible being; the supreme governor, and disposer of events. Of this ruling intelligence they judged that matter is the corporeal frame, and affirmed that its parts are obsequious to his will, in the same manner as the various members of the human form are spontaneously compliant to the spirit that resides in it*. Now, as the maintainers of these principles acknowledged at the same time the existence and prevalence of evil, it is obvious that this effect can be traced, according to their principles, to no other cause than Jupiter himself. For it would, as Plutarch observes, be grossly absurd to say, that the world is an animal of which this Being is the soul, and to deny at the same time that it is subject to his will. We might say with equal truth, that in the same animal the legs might move the tongue to speak, and the horns strike in opposition to that impulse whereby those members are universally governed. If therefore the parts of the universe be thus obsequious to the will or influence of Jupiter as the spirit that presides in it, he must be accountable for their

* Plutarch. ubi sup. and p. 1075.

motions and disposition, as well as for their consequences; and is thus, in the strictest sense of that term, *the author of evil*. But this doctrine the author above mentioned justly reprobates, as altogether unworthy the Supreme Intelligence, in whom it is much better to say, that power or knowledge is deficient, than to ascribe to him *, with both in their greatest extent, all the crimes that are committed in the world, and the misery whereof they are the causes.

From the preceding account of the tenets of this celebrated sect of philosophers on the present important subject, it must be acknowledged, that the charge of maintaining absurd and inconsistent principles is proved against them by incontestable evidence. God, in their estimation, is at one time the fate or destiny, to whose decrees at another he is said to be subjected †. He is in the same manner the greatest and best Being, who will finally exterminate evil from his workmanship ‡. This evil which subsists necessarily as being opposite to good, may yet be abolished; while that which is con-

---

* Id. p. 1076.

† Necessitas et Deos alligat. Senec: Fieri igitur omnia Fato, ratio coget fateri. Cicer. de Divinat. Lib. i. cap. 55.

‡ Plutarch. ubi sup.

trary

trary to it, and exists by being contrary, will continue to have influence *: finally, Jupiter, who wills only what is good, is the soul of the universe, by whose will all its parts are directed †: yet to this *good* being we must ascribe, according to their hypothesis, all the evil, both physical and moral that prevails in the world; unless we should consider him as unable to regulate the movements of a machine, wherein, as the ruling spirit, he constantly operates.

Absurd and repugnant to each other as the stoical dogmas on the doctrine of the origin of evil, which have been enumerated, appear to be, these are yet founded upon a principle, whereof ancient and modern philosophers have equally availed themselves in their examination of this question, and have inculcated almost universally in their writings. To the difficulty of reconciling the establishments of necessity with that freedom whereby they seem to be counteracted, we must ascribe declarations that are apparently opposite in the works of the ancients ‡. Perhaps

---

* Id. ibid.

† Αυτοι δε των κακων Αρχην ΑΓΑΘΟΝ οντα τον θεον ποιουσι· Ου γαρ, η γε υλη το κακον εξ εαυτης παρισχηκεν, Plutarch 1076.

‡ Thus Plato himself, who so strenuously maintains, as we have already seen, the superintendency of Providence, yet assigns, in seeming opposition to this doctrine, the disposal

haps the best method of accounting for passages of this import is to consider these in general as relating in their first and ultimate sense to the immutability of the divine nature and decrees, of which the term Fate is particularly expressive; and in a secondary and subordinate acceptation, to the aspect of things according to our imperfect and limited comprehension, wherein chance and blind impulse appear to dispose of them at pleasure.

I cannot more properly sum up the various theories of ancient writers on the origin of evil,

posal of many occurrences to chance and fortune. Θνητων μεν μηδενα νεμοθετειν μηδεν, Τυχας δε ειναι σχεδην απαντα τα ανθρωπινα πραγματα. De Legib. lib. x. Plutarch in the same spirit adopts, in the following passage, the doctrine of Epicurus, and censures both Plato and Anaxagoras, of whom he approves at all other times, even when defending contrary principles, for differing from him in this instance in opinion. Κοινως ουν αμαρτανουσιν αμφοτεροι οτι τον θεον εποιησαν επιστρεφομενον των ανθρωπινων, η και τουτο χαριν τον κοσμον κατασκευαζοντα. Oper. v. ii. p. 881. In these words our author obviously defends the dogma of Epicurus, whose Gods, residing constantly in heaven, took no concern whatever in the business of mankind. These and many other examples of a similar nature that might be produced, when considered as evidences of human fallibility and imperfection, are incontestible proofs of the necessity and use of revelation in opening a path through the labyrinth wherein the greatest geniuses of antiquity have found themselves bewildered.

before

before entering into the Platonic doctrine, than in the words of Sallust the philosopher. Those events, says he, which the power of God conducts, beyond our expectation, towards a good purpose, we ascribe (*unjustly*) to Fortune. Let us not therefore wonder when we observe that bad men prosper in life, and that the virtuous are poor and depressed *; for riches have the highest value in the judgment of the former, and in that of the latter are of no estimation. Prosperity cannot subdue in a bad man the passions that must render him miserable, and the good find in the practice of virtue an adequate and constant reward †.

3. In explaining the causes that are assigned by Plato, as being adequate to the production of evil, I must take leave of the philosopher whom I have hitherto followed in his refutation of Zeno and Epicurus; as he appears to have erred in detailing the principles of Plato on this subject, which he represents to coincide with those

---

* Πολλοι τοι πλυτεισι κακοι αγαθοι δε πενονται. Hesiod.

† Η τοινυν τα διαφορα, και τα παρ ελπιδα γινομενα προς αγαθον ταττουσα Δυναμις, την Θεαν, ΤΥΧΗ νομιζεσθαι. Ειδε κακοι ευτυχωσιν, αγαθοι δε πενονται, θαυμαζον ου δει. Οι μεν γαρ παντα, οι δε ουδενος πλντα ποιησι. και των μεν κακων η ευτυχια ουκ αν αφελοι την κακιαν, ταις δε αγαθοις η αρετη μονη αρεσκει. De Diis et Mundo, Ap. Opusc. Mythol. p. 20.

of Zoroaster. On his judgment in this case, it is here proper to make some observations.

Plutarch, who seems himself to have favoured this doctrine, was no doubt ambitious of supporting it by the authority of our great philosopher. He produces with this purpose various passages from his writings, but founds his charge principally on one doctrine, of which we shall examine the tenor.

Plato, after having related a fable concerning an original revolution of the heavenly bodies, very different from the present, in the dialogue entitled Politicus, makes the following remark: " Although the world derives life and immortality from its great artificer, it may yet revolve, when deprived of his influence, in a course opposite to that which was originally prescribed to it, in consequence of the ungovernable disposition of the ruling spirit by whom it is agitated *." To this spirit he gives, says Plutarch, the name necessity, and ascribes to it that disorderly motion which took place among the parts of matter before the formation of the world †. According therefore to his commentator, our author taught, that this being or spirit

* Plat. p. 527.
† De Creat. Anim. Oper. v. ii. p. 1014.

endea-

endeavours at all times to re-establish the primary habit or tendency of those parts, and counteracts in this manner the purpose of the wise and good Creator of all things *. Here then, two hostile and independent sovereigns appear to preside in the universe; and we cease to contemplate with astonishment the evils that prevail in it, when they are considered as the effects of a mighty contest between powers, whose characters are not more opposite than their influence is universal. I make the following remarks, in order to vindicate our author from the charge that is here brought against him.

1. It must be obvious to any person who has considered the preceding account of the dogmas of Plato, that he could not have adopted the tenets of Zoroaster without lying open to the imputation of inconsistence. An incontestable proof of this truth was given in the various passages of his writings, that ascertain his belief of the divine unity, to which the reader is referred for satisfaction †. They who would render this doctrine consistent with the notion of a good and an evil principle, will find insuperable difficulty in proving, that a Being who is *one* (an idea that excludes equality;) can be success-

* Ibid. p. 1015.
† Sect. i. pass.

fully

fully opposed by a spirit of inferior order, whose purposes, the intelligence must be limited that does not detect, and the power circumscribed, that is not adequate to restrain. Plato therefore, who considers both as being *perfectly* united in *one* object, cannot maintain the opinion which Plutarch ascribes to him, consistently with truths which we have seen that he inculcates.

2. The words which this philosopher quotes from the writings of our author with the present purpose, do not justify the conclusion which he draws from them. For, although it be true that Plato represents the order of nature as being disturbed by the motions of a perverse and unquiet spirit, yet he attributes this perturbation to the absence of the Δημιουργος, or Creator; and he describes the period of his absence, as being marked by an unnatural revolution of the heavenly bodies, and by the miseries that arise from it *.

3. Plutarch has either omitted to mention through inadvertency, or has wilfully overlooked a passage of the same dialogue, that is wholly opposite to the doctrine of Zoroaster. " Let

---

* Του παντος ο μεν Κυβερνητης ,πεδαλιων οιακος αφεμενος, εις την εαυτου περιωπην απεστη· Τον δε κοσμον παλιν ανεστρεφεν Ερμαρμενη, και ξυμφυτη επιθυμια. p. 538.

us not, says Plato, believe, that two Gods of contrary natures turn the world in various and opposite directions *." These words are indeed so decisive of our author's sentiments on this subject, that the reader may judge the preceding part of the vindication to have been superfluous. It is however of material consequence to obviate a misconceived opinion, before I proceed to explain the real principles of Plato, which leads to a wrong notion of them. And I am solicitous to prove, that he is at all times consistent in his account of the first cause, as it has already been rendered evident, that the appellation ΘΕΟΣ, God, characterizes in his writings the author of all good things, excluding every claim to equality or independence.

Having thus examined Plutarch's account of our author's doctrine on the present subject, it remains, that we should explain the principles upon which he attempts to answer the question concerning the origin of evil.

A reader of common observation must be impressed by the modesty and apparent diffidence wherewith Plato enters into this inquiry. In

---

* Εκ παντων δε των τουτων, τον κοσμον μητι αυτον χρη φαιναι στρεφειν εαυτον αει, μητε δι ΔΥΟ τινε θια φρονουντε εαυτοις εναντια στρεφειν αυτον. p. 536.

his

his Timæus, he disclaims dogmatical assertion on a subject that has given occasion to so many theories, and guards us against being disappointed by finding his account of the matter as those of former philosophers, exceptionable and imperfect. " Let us remember, O Socrates, says this speaker, that as *men* our enquiries must be bounded by probability. Certainty lies beyond our reach *."

In order to lay before the reader a full account of our author's observations and reasonings on the causes of evil, it is proper to remark, that the sphere within which it has influence, is, according to him, only a small part of the universe. Its operation is limited to beings who are subjected to mortality, and to those inferior regions of which they are inhabitants †. The pure residence of Deity remains at all times uncontaminated by pollution, in the same manner as the divine nature, which is wholly unsusceptible of this impression ‡.

---

* Tim. p. 1057. et Laert. Pluton.

† Αλλ' ουτ'απολλισθαι τα κακα δυνατον, ιυτ' ιν Θεοις· αυτα ιδρυσθαι· Την δε θνητην φυσιν, και τον των τοπον περιπολει εξ Αναγκης. Thæet. p. 129.

‡ ΘΕΟΣ ουδαμη ιυδαμως αδικος, αλλως οιον τε δικαιοτατος. &c. ibid.

In

In the space wherein evil predominates, Plato farther taught, that its existence is *necessary*. Evils, he says, necessarily (εξ ΑΝΑΓΚΗΣ) surround the dwellings and habitations of mortals *. This term is made use of, as we shall see immediately, partly with the purpose of vindicating the Supreme Being from the charge of admitting these blemishes into his works, and partly as relating to causes that are afterwards enumerated.

Those two points therefore being established, what, it will be inquired, are the sources wherein this effect, destructive of order, government, and happiness, has its original? I answer, the following are those which he assigns as being adequate to this purpose.

1. The *imperfection* of man, the *necessary* consequence of his being created, and subordinate.

2. That tendency which the parts of matter retain in all forms and situations, to return to that unquiet and agitated state wherein they were originally involved.

3. The effect of matter upon the spirit, or immaterial substance wherewith it is united in the human form, so as to constitute man.

* Id. ibid.

Our author adds to this enumeration of the causes of evil, that it is upon the whole productive of good in many cases, and that to a good man all evils will finally be beneficial.

1. The imperfection of man is so obviously one cause of natural evil, that a late learned and ingenious writer considers this circumstance as alone sufficient to account for its admission *. This tenet of Plato is the same as the peripatetic principle of *privation*, which is illustrated so particularly by Aristotle and his followers. This *negation*, as it may be termed, is said by him to imply a deficiency, whereby a creature being necessarily imperfect, is subjected as necessarily to certain evils. Without entering into all the distinctions of this acute metaphysician on the present subject, (De Natur. auscult. Lib. i. c. 10.) we may consider it as equal to the production of those effects which he ascribes to it. For nothing can be more plain, than that if God, as a perfect Being, is exempted from evil; man, as an imperfect creature, is certainly exposed to its influence. In fact, it is from the imperfection of our nature that temptation derives its efficacy. This term, which has no meaning when applied to the Supreme Intelli-

* King's Origin of Evil.

gence, who comprehends a whole, is the fruitful source of evil to creatures who see only a part.

Although our author does not enter so closely into this matter as Aristotle, by using distinction and definition, he yet traces up the evils of life at great length, in various parts of his writings, to their causes in human weakness and imperfection. With this purpose, after having traced the passions, fear, anger, love, &c. to their cause, as we shall see afterwards, in the union of matter and spirit, he adds, that those alone are acceptable to God, who, by a strenuous effort, conquer these passions, which propel them to the commission of evil*. In the same spirit he represents this propensity as an effect of that inability to govern ourselves, which indicates the imperfection of our nature and faculties, and which the good are in some degree enabled to overcome †. Have you not observed, says he, how acutely the little souls of those who are bad, although they are denominated wise men, discern the objects to which their sight is turned, when they are compelled, as it were, to be the slaves of depravity? Evil dispositions keep pace

* Tim. p. 1055.
† De Legib. l. i. p. 781.

in the hearts of those men with the acuteness and ardour of this contemplation *.

To him who considers natural evil as originating in this manner in human imperfection, our author was aware, that the question would naturally be suggested, What are the causes of those peculiar characters of imperfection and of depravity, so strongly and so particularly marked, whereby the world and its inhabitants are distinguished?—The answer to this query introduces a position which may be termed the foundation of the Platonic reasonings on these subjects, that the parts of matter which were originally unquiet and agitated, have at all times a propension to return to their primitive disorder.

2. That we may fully comprehend the theory of Plato, as far as the present subject is concerned, the reader must call to remembrance our account of the Ὕλη or first matter, whereof all things were framed, as being compounded of every elementary substance †. We have seen that the forms of this mass, turbid and fluc-

---

* The Greek word here is Ψυχαριον, of which even the Latin term animula does not convey the full import, as the latter is expressive of affection and the former of contempt.

† See Sect. iii. pass.

tuating in their first state, were brought into order by the Author of Nature, who, in accomplishing this purpose, is emphatically said to have made use of numbers, proportion, and harmony *. Although the Creator, in carrying his purpose into execution, rendered his work exact and beautiful, he yet did not deprive matter of its original tendency to inquietude and agitation, which our great philosopher sometimes terms, an innate aptitude or propensity to motion, not destitute of spirit; and sometimes, as we have seen, a restless and turbulent mind, opposite to that of the beneficent Maker †. The substance therefore whereof the world, and man its principal inhabitant, is framed, retains the character or impression which it originally received; and it is to this quality that he principally refers when he mentions the *mind* containing the passions and grosser appetites which inferior deities placed in the heart of man, whose inordinate motions are always opposed to those of a pure and unbiassed understanding.

Of this representation the obvious consequence is, that as Omnipotence was exerted in the ori-

---

* Αλλ' υσης (υλης) ιι παθισι παντοδαποις και μιταβολαις αταϰτοις, ιξιιλι την πολλην αορεστιαν και πλημμιλιιαν Αρμονια, και Αναλογια, και Ρυθμω. Plut. v. ii. p. 1015.

† Ψυχην ιναντιον και αντιπαλον το Αγαθουργν. Id. ibid.

ginal

ginal task of bringing order out of confusion, by framing the universe according to a noble and beautiful pattern, such as it is said to have been fashioned, so its influence was exerted with peculiar efficacy during the first ages in maintaining that harmony which it had established, and to which the parts of matter are repugnant. Our author's theory of the present subject will appear to some advantage after these previous observations.

God, therefore, who is himself the fountain of all excellence, framed the world after his own image, according to the Platonic doctrine, without any appearance of evil. So far it will be allowed on all hands, that this tenet is consonant to that of the Jewish legislator, who teaches, that the work in its first state was worthy of that Being who is the source of beauty and perfection *. In the same spirit our philosopher taught, that, to a world thus constituted, the Supreme Being adapted perfect inhabitants, of whom himself condescended to be the guardian and the guide †. His description of this simple and happy race, wandering in naked innocence over the earth, and feeding upon the fruits and herbage which it yielded spontaneously, presents

* Tim. ubi sup.
† Id. ibid. and Polit. p. 537. De Legib. l. iv. p. 831.

before

before imagination the first pair, enjoying the productions, and reclining in the bowers of Paradise; sometimes permitted to converse with the Author of their existence, and sometimes with angels, as the companions, as well as conductors of their walks and occupations *.

The Creator of all things having now accomplished his purpose, and peopled heaven and earth with inhabitants, ceased, at a certain period, to counteract the innate tendencies of matter, by the immediate exertion of his omnipotence, and permitted that these tendencies (under certain laws that limit their influence) should produce their natural effects. At whatever time this change took place in the universe, the voice of antiquity leads us to consider it as having certainly happened. It is to this revolution that our author alludes, when he represents the world and its inhabitants as having passed from the peaceful reign of Saturn, wherein the inhabitants were blessed with propitious seasons, and with unceasing abundance, to that of Jupiter and the inferior deities. Violent concussions, that shook the frame of the world and deformed its beauty, are said upon this occasion to have announced his departure. These changes declared, not that evil then originated, but that its influence, sup-

* Genes. iii. 8.

pressed

pressed under the former establishment, was rendered conspicuous. It was at the time when this disorder subsided, and the world again performed its accustomed revolution, that men became sensible of the change that has taken place in the order of things; an alteration, which, although it seems to threaten universal dissolution, will not accomplish it. God will return at last from his retirement, and, reassuming the reins of government, will put an end for ever to old age and death*.

From the different circumstances of this detail brought into one point of view, the following principles appear to be those which our author assigns as the causes of evil: 1. As the operation of evil is circumscribed within the inferior region that is occupied by imperfect beings, many kinds of it, being essentially and necessarily connected with imperfection, adhere (if we may thus express it) to the nature of the agent, and cannot even in thought be separated from the idea of his existence. 2. As evils of some kinds have their original in the nature of man, others arise as necessarily from the substance whereof his body is compounded. Although the Author of all things was actuated in

* Platon. Polit.

framing

framing the universe by a general benevolence, whereby he was prompted to impart some portion of his own felicity to his creatures, yet in creating MATTER he formed something opposite to his own incorporeal nature, and necessarily endowed with contrary qualities. 3. The influence of those qualities was at first repressed by the Maker, who was willing to render his creatures happy during the first ages, by an immediate and unremitted exertion of his omnipotence. 4. Nothing more is understood by the retirement of the Supreme Agent from government than his permission, at a certain period, that things should proceed in their natural course, when the effect of matter upon the spirit, with which it is united, is forcibly represented by the agitation that prevailed universally, and by the immediate appearance of physical evil. 5. I observe, in the last place, that at the time abovementioned, when matter reassumed the habit that is essential to it, man, whose pure spirit is disturbed by its influence, felt the powerful effects of passions and appetites that corresponded to the external perturbations of nature, and arose from the structure of material organization.

3. Upon the whole, therefore, it is in the union of matter and spirit that we find the cause of

of those evils which we ascribe to human passions and propensities; and in the tendency of the first principles of things to agitation and disorder, we mark the origin of those subsequent commotions to which they are subjected. Plato denominates evils of the former kind, Δεινα και αναγκεα παθηματα, terrible and necessary perturbations: the latter we have seen that he attributes sometimes to innate propensity, and sometimes to a spirit εναντιη το Αγαθουργω opposite to the beneficent Maker, perhaps by a bold and significant prosopopeia.

In answer therefore to the question of Plutarch, by what means matter that has no efficacy in itself should be the cause of evil? I observe, that our author no where says that it is the case. He mentions, as we have already seen, that evil is a consequence necessarily arising from the union of body and spirit, and as the term whereby we denote an effect whereof this coalition is at all times productive; otherwise, the unquiet state of the parts of matter in their original situation, and the turbulence of unruly elements whereby this inquietude is maintained, could not properly have been denominated evils as long as there was no percipient to feel or suffer by this commotion. The spirit (if any spirit there were) who raised the tumult, had pleasure in its continuance;

continuance; and by us those circumstances are deemed to be pernicious only in consequence of our particular feelings and perceptions.

But whence you inquire, arise injustice, oppression, discord, calumny, the waste of ambition, the insult of pride, the grasping of avarice, and the purpose of malevolence?—From passions, in the opinion of Plato, that have their seat in the heart of man, and correspond in their violence and effects to the elements that lay waste his habitation *. His body, compounded of material substances, is exposed to natural evils, which affect its inhabitant; and the soul, of which God is the immediate author, governs appetite and brutal impulse, without being able at all times to counteract their influence. Evil therefore arises necessarily from this union of matter and spirit, and from the imperfection of that being who is constituted by their union.

The preceding detail will suggest two questions to an intelligent reader, whereof our author appears to have been aware; and it is proper to examine what he has said in answer to both. The first respects the causes of the present unequal distribution of reward and punishment:

* Plat. p. 1073.

the

the second regards the reasons for which souls are sent down into this region of sorrow and vicissitude, from mansions wherein they enjoyed supreme and uninterrupted felicity. He, to whom the former question is suggested by the contemplation of the divine administration, will argue in the following manner.

Granting, he will say, that the causes of evil that have been assigned should be equal to the production of this effect, even under the government of a beneficent Being, whence is it that his conduct in the order of things appears sometimes to be regulated by caprice, and sometimes to be dictated by malevolence?—It is apparently capricious, because we discover in it few marks of rational choice, or indications of equal and judicious distribution; on the other hand, it is seemingly malevolent, when we recollect some among many examples of benefits conferred on mean and unworthy persons; of the reward of virtue being withheld, and of ungrateful returns to deeds of generosity and beneficence that pass without animadversion of any kind.

I shall examine in the subsequent section, the use which our author makes of the present unequal and defective arrangement, as being the evidence

evidence of a future and more equal dispensation. We are called upon at present to follow him in his account of a preceding scene, wherein those who believe the Platonic doctrine on this subject, will find an answer to their question.

Whether men, who had recourse to the doctrine of pre-existence in vindicating the conduct of Providence, received it originally by supernatural communication, or confided in it implicitly as delivered by legislators and philosophers; whether their knowledge of natural religion was greater, as they were deficient in that of revelation; or finally, whether they were endowed with some portion of that *reminiscence*, of whose reality they appear to have conviction; it is yet certain, that a belief of this doctrine obtained among the ancients at a very early period, and that it even obtained credit among fathers in the first ages of the church. I shall make some observations on this latter testimony, after having examined our author's account of this tenet, and of the purpose to which it is applied.

The method of inculcating the most essential truths by entertaining narrations, or beautiful apologues, although not peculiarly characteristical of our great philosopher, is however practised by him upon all occasions, and seems indeed

deed to have been congenial to his creative and exuberant imagination. Of the truth of this remark, the present subject exhibits an evidence that demands particular regard.

Of narratives that claim attention in consequence of their singularity, that of ER, the Armenian, (whom Socrates calls an illustrious man;) is undoubtedly one of the most extraordinary in all its circumstances which we meet with in the records of mankind. Many readers will, perhaps, find difficulty in discovering, whether our philosopher ought to be considered in this matter as relating a fact, or as inventing an apologue*. But be that as it may, it will be acknowledged on all hands, that its ultimate tendency is to evince the wisdom of God, and the impartiality of his various dispensations.

* It may not be improper to observe here, that in the judgment of Origen, Plato related the story as a fact, to which his followers also appear to have given credit: for in his refutation of the cavils of Celsus, he refers the heathen who found difficulty in believing the doctrine of a resurrection, to the story of our Armenian, as a proof that this tenet was adopted by Plato. And he mentions with the same purpose, a similar tale recorded by Heraclitus. Επι δε περι της αναϛασιω; Ιησȣ χριϛȣ χλιυαζȣσιν οι απιϛοι, παραθησομεθα μεν και πλατωνα λεγοντα, ΗΡΟΝ τον αρμενιον, μετα δωδεκα ημεραις εκ της πυρας εγεγερθαι, και απηγγελκεναι τα περι των ιϛ ΑΔΟΝ. Cont. Cel. Lib. ii. p. 70.

On

On the tenth day, after a battle wherein this Armenian had fallen, his body, when drawn from the heap of putrid carcasses, was found to be uncorrupted; and on the twelfth, when it was laid on the funeral pile, was reanimated; the man being rendered capable to relate the transactions of the interval between the time of his supposed death, and resurrection.

The two principal circumstances of his narrative are the following. 1. The souls of those who ascend from earth, and of those who descend from superior regions to reoccupy mortal bodies, meet together on a spacious field or meadow, where they converse during seven days, on the subject of terrestrial occurrences. 2. The latter after this conference, are prepared for their mortal states, by drinking the water of Lethe, which expels from their minds all remembrance of the past. The journey of four days, which these spirits then undertake to meet the arbiters of fate; the pillar of light, which they behold descending from heaven to earth; the right orbs of the celestial sphere revolving around the spindle of NECESSITY; the three daughters of FATE, seated on thrones, clothed in white robes, and singing as they weave the varied texture of events; of the present, the past, and the future, are incidents exquisitely

beau-

beautiful, of which that mind must be void of sensibility which does not feel the impression. They approach at last to Lachesis, from whose knees a prophet snatching the lots and tablets of human events, and holding these up to view, addresses the beings assembled before him in the name of the goddess, in words to the following import.

" Ye spirits of one day, destinate to a mortal state which must speedily be terminated by death, know that the Dæmon, or minister of fate, who must wait upon you during life, is not permitted to select the person whom he is appointed to accompany, you must make a choice for yourselves. He who draws the first lot, first chooses the life to which by the irrevocable decree of destiny, he must afterwards adhere. Virtue alone is under no restraint. Those who participate of her favour, or hope to be benefited by her influence, will share of both, according to the degree of estimation wherein she is held by him. The fault is that of him who chooseth. God is without blame *."

The reader will perceive, that the question concerning the inequality of present distribution,

* De Reput. lib. x. p. 761.

is answered in the circumstantial detail above mentioned upon the following grounds; 1. What in our opinion is culpable inequality, assumes this appearance, merely because we are unacquainted with the particulars of a preceding series of events, whereby the divine perfections are fully vindicated, according to our author, in the moral government of the universe. 2. In order to understand the nature of this arrangement, our attention is called to a doctrine by no means improbable in the opinion of Plato, and confirmed in his judgment, by an actual revelation. This doctrine is, that the soul of man, instead of being created at the instant when it enters into the body, descends, on the contrary, at that time from some superior region, and takes the consequence of the lot which it draws, as well as of the guardian ordained to be its attendant. 3. According to our author's principles, fate and free-will are reconciled; the former as having fixed irreversible establishments; the latter as possessing an original freedom of choice among objects that are placed before it, although not the power of resuming a selection once made, or of altering the series or order of events. 4. When we consider that the state and circumstances wherein we are placed will terminate in a translation to our original and native regions; we are induced, not merely to acquiesce under our present trial and chastisement, as consequences that are attendant in our present situation, but to look forward to that period with animated hope, when we shall obtain, by the exercise of perseverance and patience, an higher station, and a more adequate reward.

I cannot dismiss this subject of pre-existence, which makes so great a figure in the writings of the ancients, as a Pythagorean * as well as a Platonic doctrine, without making some remarks on a congenial opinion from which our knowledge of the former is judged principally to be derived. This is the tenet of reminiscence, a faculty wherein science, in the judgment of the wisest ancients, is said to have its origin.

Our author, in the same manner as Pythagoras, is so thoroughly convinced of the pre-existence of the human mind, that he lays down as a fundamental principle, of which he endeavours to establish the truth, that all knowledge originates in the remembrance of past transactions; so that to learn, and to remember, are

* Nos dixit Pythagoras, quasi in mercatus quandam celebritatem, ex urbe aliqua, sic *in hanc vitam* ex *alia vita & natura* profectos alios gloriæ servire, &c. Cicer. Oper. v. iii. p. 393.

terms

terms of the same import *. With this purpose Plato makes some ingenious observations, tending to prove that our present ideas are only transcripts of certain originals that existed in a former state, of which reflection must ascertain to us the reality. Concerning knowledge in general he remarks, that at the time when our senses present their objects before us, we not only have some intuitive discernment of their nature, but that dissimilar things bring each other immediately into view. Thus the sight of an harp presents an image of the man who possesses, or of the musician who useth it; and the same effect will be produced by a well executed drawing of the instrument. This is what Plato denominates remembrance; and he considers the original patterns and exemplars of all as having existed and been impressed upon the mind in a former state, and as being brought before it by this faculty in the present.

As a principal illustration of the Platonic dogma respecting a state of pre-existence, our philosopher has recourse to an abstracted idea which the mind conceives of equality; whereof, as a specimen, at the same time of philosophical

---

* Ἡ Μάθησις οὐκ ἀλλο ἢ ΑΝΑΜΝΗΣΙΣ τυγχανει ἐστι; και κατα τυτο αναγκη πυ τμας; εν προτερω τινι χρονω μεμαθηκεναι α νυν αναμιμνησκομεθα. Τετομεν αδυνατον ει μη ην που ημων η Ψυχη πριν εν τω τε ανθρωπινω ειδει γενεσθαι. Phæd. p. 195.

acumen, and of the most refined ingenuity, I shall endeavour to exhibit a representation,

Equality Plato considers in two lights, as being either sensible or intellectual. Sensible equality (as it may be termed) is that which we perceive to take place between objects of equal powers or dimensions. By the term intellectual equality, on the contrary, he understands that abstracted idea of it which the mind, he says, has gained by remembrance, and is the standard whereby we judge concerning equality either of objects of sense, or of qualities intellectual or moral. This standard our author represents as being much more accurate than that of which we have examples. Thus I can form an idea of wisdom, sanctity, &c. to which no pattern, wherewith I am acquainted, perfectly corresponds; and I can in thought conceive, that the mind may possess any or all of those excellencies in a degree of perfect uniformity of which experience is not the parent. Now whence, says he, is this notion of a *perfect* standard, conceived amidst *imperfect* objects, and inconsistent with present experience, derived? Incompatible as it is with whatever our thoughts and senses offer in this state to our observation, it must have been derived from circumstances with which we have been acquainted in a preceding one. It has

has its origin therefore, according to the Platonic theory, in *remembrance*. We recollect upon this occasion the past, instead of reasoning from the present; and in this manner a standard of excellence is made known to us in our present situation, to which nothing whereof we have cognisance perfectly corresponds.

I am aware that it may be objected to this argument, that although it should be granted that we have an idea of perfect excellence, of which, as being imperfect creatures, we cannot produce an adequate imitation; it does not follow that this idea has therefore been gained in a pre-existent state, and that it is brought to the mind by remembrance. The intellect, it will be said, ascends towards the orginal by progressive steps, and appears to exert no other power in all this process than that of arranging objects that are supplied by experience. This guide does not, indeed, conduct us to the period at which we wish to arrive; but she leaves us at a period when we can frame to ourselves the present abstracted idea of equality, by the simple operation of excluding in thought from the various models that are placed before us, whatever appears to be faulty or inaccurate.

A Platonist, in replying to this objection, would acknowledge that it has weight when we con-

consider merely the nature of subordinate agents, of the perfection of which we obtain an idea by the method above-mentioned: but he would observe, that when we substitute the term *perfection* in its strict sense, as being applied to the Supreme Being, in place of the word *equality*, which has the same import, our conception of that supreme excellence is that abstracted idea which in Plato's estimation is not derived from experience. It cannot be said that we gain the knowledge, as far as we have any knowledge of this absolute perfection, merely by the act of excluding, in thought from one model the faults and inaccuracies which we have observed to be prevalent in others. The mind ascends in this process towards the great Original of all things, without being restrained in its effort or bounded in its research. And it is the thought that wanders through infinity, while it is employed in this sublime contemplation, of which Plato pronounces, that having existed in a former state in the highest comprehension, its objects are faintly presented by remembrance in the present.

To our author's observations on this subject it is only proper to add here, that by believing that the souls of men have pre-existed, we avoid the supposition of an uninterrupted exertion of of creative energy employed in producing these at the instant of original animation; an argument which, no doubt, had principal weight with Origen, and other of the later Platonists, who embraced this tenet of our great philosopher.

I have thus far entered into the metaphysic of Plato, in explaining a doctrine which is so conspicuous among his theological tenets, that it could not be illustrated without a deduction of this nature. In the belief of pre-existence, it must be acknowledged, that the mind finds an easy and pleasing solution of difficulties which embarras its researches upon any other hypothesis, and prevent it from establishing any positive conclusion. Notwithstanding these advantages, however enforced by all the learning and ingenuity of a celebrated modern writer, I cannot think, that it is either consonant to the institutions and spirit of Christianity, or sufficiently authenticated by the declarations of scripture. I shall here make some observations on the only passages of the inspired writings that appear to give authority to it, in order to compleat our view of the subject. Of these, one is in the Old, and another in the New Testament. In the former we meet with the following words, in the address of the Supreme Being to the prophet Jeremiah, " Before I formed thee in the belly,

I *knew*

I *knew* thee." These words, which imply that God knew the prophet before he existed in the present state, seem to have reference to his knowledge of him in that which preceded it. Commentators, indeed, understand the passage as being expressive of the divine appointment of Jeremiah to officiate in a certain character and department. And this most probably is its true import. Yet to the present interpretation, the following objections may be urged with some plausibility.

1. The term I *knew* thee conveys a much stronger meaning than the word *appointed*, which would be substituted in its place, the former referring to some state wherein acquaintance was contracted; and the latter implying nothing more than the decisive purpose or determination of an agent. 2. A distinction, it may be said, seems to be made in the passage itself between God's knowledge of the prophet, and his appointment or destination of him to the prophetical office. " Before I formed thee in the belly, I *knew* thee; and before thou camest forth out of the womb, I sanctified thee and ordained thee, &c." The advocate of the Platonic doctrine on this subject would consider the following as the import of this declaration: Before I formed thee in the belly, I knew thee

in

in thy pre-existent state; and when thou descendedst into thy present habitation, and wast yet in the womb, I ordained thee to exercise the prophetical office among the nations.

The second passage, wherein there appears to be a tacit acknowledgment of this doctrine, is that in John ix. 2, where the disciples refer to their master the following celebrated question concerning the blind man who was brought to him: " Who did sin, this man or his parents, that he was *born* blind?" On this question the following remarks would most probably be made by one inclined to believe in the doctrine of pre-existence.

1. It will occur to an attentive reader, that this Pythagorean tenet was received, not merely by a particular sect, but by the Jews in general; because it is mentioned without hesitation as being universally prevalent. Accordingly we learn from Josephus, that this opinion was prevalent among the Essenes, a well-known sect*; and it was very probably derived from the Jews of Alexandria, and spread by their means among their brethren in Judea, according the conjecture of an ingenious commentator †.

* De Bell. Judaic. l. ii. c. 12. † Whitby, ap Loc.

2. No

2. No doubt can obtain respecting the meaning of the question; for if the man was *born blind* as the punishment of sin, it must have been of a sin that was committed in some state that preceded his birth; and the question implies, that we may suffer in our present sphere of action, in the opinion of those men, for sins of which we were guilty in a former one.

3. If by the term disciples we understand here the chosen twelve who accompanied Jesus in all his ministrations, it will follow, that they had been permitted to maintain this principle without having been opposed in their belief, to say the least of it, by their master; who, far from reprobating the notion in his answer, seems, on the contrary, tacitly to approve it. Neither hath *this man sinned*, nor his parents, &c. In these words it is obvious that the justification of the man from the charge of having sinned before he was born is a direct answer to the question of the disciples, and that it contains an acknowledgement of the possibility of the event.

4. A maintainer of this dogma would further urge in defence of it, that whether it may or may not bear to be denominated properly scriptural, it is adopted in an apocryphal book by the

the author of the wisdom of Solomon, whose words are, ch. viii. v. 20. "Being good, he came into a body undefiled, or free from any notable infirmity." We have already seen, that the air, according to the mythology of the ancients, was peopled with innumerable spiritual beings*, of whom those who inhabit regions that are contiguous to the earth, return back to mortal bodies, wherein they *wish*, according to Philo †, or in the judgment of Plato, are *compelled*, to reside ‡.

After all, I do not mention these passages, of which the meaning is ambiguous, as direct proofs that this doctrine is justified by the authority of scripture, or can be considered as an article of revealed religion.

Thus far I have examined our author's solution of the question concerning the present unequal distribution of reward and punishment.

---

* Hence arose the occupation of Exorcists, as they were termed, a business in which old women were employed, who, by reading certain verses, and performing particular ceremonies, were supposed to drive away spirits who frequented houses, and terrified the inhabitants.

Et veniet quæ lustret anus, lectumque locumque,
Præferet & tremula sulphur et ova manu.
      Ovid. de Art. Amand. l. 2.

† De Somn. p. 455.   ‡ Platon. p. 1223.

But

But that we may have a full view of his principles on this subject, it is proper, that in examining the second branch of our enquiry, we should mention the causes for which, according to the Platonic hypothesis, souls are sent down into a region of sorrow and vicissitude, from mansions wherein they enjoyed supreme and uninterrupted felicity. I have already marked and exemplified our author's method of seizing imagination while he informs the understanding, in illustrating the maxims of his sublime philosophy. In answering the present interrogatory, we must follow him once more through the incidents of a narrative, wherein he assigns the causes of this degradation, and of the consequences that arise from it.

Our spirits, says he, unlike the Gods who are perfect beings, are actuated by desires, which in the same manner as horses of unequal temperament, yoked in a chariot, pull different ways, and destroy each other's influence. These are the love of pleasure and of virtue, of which the latter leads to the noblest attainments. When Jupiter therefore conducts the inferior deities to the highest celestial elevation, he is followed with ease by such beings as himself, who feel no impediment in the ascent; but by others with more difficulty. In these every nobler

passion

passion is counterpoised by the desire of sensual enjoyment. Becoming therefore gradually assimilated to those whom they contemplate with satisfaction, they are no longer as their companions, entertained and enraptured by beholding justice, temperance, and science, not merely as ideal forms, but as objects that exist in the divine mind. The *wings* of the soul (as they are termed by Plato with great beauty and significance,) i. e. the desires whereby it ascends to the fountain of happiness, are impaired in this manner, and finally are broken. The inhabitants therefore of superior regions fall down upon earth, where they act in characters that are accommodated to their dispositions and degrees of intelligence. Hence arise philosophers, heroes, legislators, poets, husbandmen, &c. according to their former knowledge and attainments *.

The purpose of Plato in this representation obviously is, to assign the reasons for which souls are sent down into their present state, and to account for the departments which they occupy. Two circumstances are the foundation of his theory. These are, that the inhabitants of etherial mansions have powers whereby they may secure felicity; and that they are free to

* Plat. ubi sup.

exercise

exercise those powers in whatever manner they may judge to be most expedient. Passions upon this hypothesis that are indulged in sensual contemplation, and desires that are permitted to wander from their great original into scenes of mortal pleasure and fruition, render those in whom they predominate proper objects of divine displeasure. They drop therefore into this world, or into the planetary orbs, as into places of punishment, or rather of purification, wherein an arrangement takes place that is conformed, not only to the present offence of the individual, but to his peculiar character and propensity. It ought also to be observed, that in the punishment, which is not final, but expiatory, strict attention is given to the justice and paternal government of the Deity; for, after a certain number of ages, the soul purified and refined in the various states through which it has passed, as metal of which the dross is left in different alembicks, returns into the regions of happiness with its nature perfectly renovated, and enters again into celestial enjoyment.

To our author's theory of this subject it has been objected, that " the justice of God does not permit that he should punish crimes of which we have no consciousness or remembrance, and which

which we cannot indeed conceive that we ever committed."

In answer to this objection I observe, 1. That it combats an ideal hypothesis: for Plato no where, as far as I know, mentions *crimes* as having been committed in a pre-existent state, or considers the evils of life as the punishment of such offences. He who is fascinated by the love of sensual pleasure, is indeed properly punished by being permitted to possess the objects of his choice: but as he is not accused of criminal excess, the consequences of this choice can be viewed only as effects of which the conduct of a free but imperfect agent is naturally productive. 2. If we should grant all that is affirmed in the objection, it will not surely follow that it is inconsistent with justice to punish a crime, merely because the criminal does not remember, or is not conscious that he committed it. Guilt could neither be extenuated nor pardoned by the plea of forgetfulness, even if we should suppose (what cannot be the case) that the Judge possessed a power of discerning the heart, and knew that there was truth in the affirmation. Divine justice may therefore punish crimes in a present state, that were committed in a preceding one.

Upon the whole, I have entered into the examination of the important and difficult inquiry concerning the origin of evil, more particularly upon the present occasion, from my desire to lay before the intelligent reader the theories of philosophers, who appear to have followed in their examination of this question the light of their own understandings, without partiality or fastidious disquisition. And after having justified Plato from a charge that is brought against him without foundation, I have endeavoured to form, from various parts of his writings, an impartial estimate of his genuine theology on this subject.

Natural evil therefore, in our author's estimation, arises from that tendency which the parts of matter, originally disordered and agitated, have at all times to return to their former fluctuation, under the influence of a power that participates of this inquietude. Moral evil, in the same manner, has its origin necessarily at present in that union of matter and spirit which constitues MAN; and of which the coalescence is productive of temporary disorder. The globe therefore which we inhabit, as well as the planetary orbs, are habitations fitted for imperfect beings, who pass from one to another in a course of expiatory trials, whereby their natures acquire

quire a likeness to that of Deity; and they find him the enjoyment of perfect felicity, as soon as this purpose is accomplished. Evil therefore is considered by Plato, as it was by his master, Pythagoras, not as a principle, but as an accident. It is a transient alienation from order and rectitude, occasioned partly by appetites of which matter is the parent, and partly by weakness and human imperfection. Goodness, on the contrary, is an essential perfection of God, which is included in our idea of his existence. Our business therefore in life is to gain a resemblance to the Divine Mind, by an imitation of his moral perfections; and to fly from this evil world, or to live apart from it as much as our nature and circumstances permit, by avoiding to be misled by its allurements, or contaminated by its impurity *.

* Thæet. p. 129.

SECTION VI.

OF THE PLATONIC DOCTRINE OF IMMORTALITY, AND OF THE NATURE OF FUTURE REWARD AND PUNISHMENT.

HISTORY, as well as the narration of travellers who have visited distant regions, are rendered at the same time entertaining and instructive, by the variety of objects which they offer to be contemplated, by the mind which investigates the rise and progress, or examines the manners and characters of nations. In the detail of the historian, it will be acknowledged, that the customs of the warlike and abstemious Spartans differed almost as widely from those of the effeminate and luxurious Asiatics; as in that of the traveller, the manners of the inhabitants of Morocco or of Tetuan, are remote from those of the people of London or Paris. Reflection will convince us, that this observation holds true, as much when it is applied to other circumstances, as to the civil customs and government of nations. The modes of worship and religious institutions of men, more especially in the early ages of society, were as different in the Pagan world, as the principles that were embraced in various parts of it, whereof specimens

mens have been exhibited in the preceding sections of this essay.

If it should be asked, whether or not, amidst an almost infinite diversity of manners, customs, prejudices, &c. there be any bond of intellectual union among mankind, (if we may thus express it;) any truth which the species without communication with each other have adopted by general intuition? I would answer, that this general axiom is the belief of a state of future existence and retribution. This concurrence, which may be regarded as the voice of mankind, this tacit acquiescence of the inhabitants of the earth in the truth of one doctrine, who are so discordant and hostile in almost all other circumstances, must impress the belief of it very powerfully upon any mind that is not steeled against its influence by the most unjustifiable arrogance and self estimation. To these passions therefore, co-operating with the love of paradox and singularity, we may ascribe most probably the conduct of a few philosophers, who have attempted to subvert a principle that is so essential to happiness; and to that dread of chastisement whereof reflection is the parent, we must in the same manner attribute the propensity that appears in men of depraved hearts, and of corresponding actions, to embrace their opinion.

opinion. The objection to the truth of this argument in behalf of a future state, that arises from the conduct of a few individuals thus actuated, does not even deserve the name of an exception; for it is in ignorant and unenlightened nations that we hear most distinctly the voice of nature. In those who boast of higher improvement and civilization this voice is stifled, at one time by occupations arising from confluence and intercourse, and at another from fastidious and laboured disquisition.

We may consider, as an evidence of the truth of these observations, that we must search for the advocates of annihilation rather among modern than ancient philosophers. Of the former, many have attempted to disseminate this comfortable doctrine: of the latter, on the contrary, who were unacquainted with the theological discoveries of modern philosophy, and who lived in times wherein the sources of enjoyment were less multiplied than at present by experiments, strenuous defenders of immortality arise on all sides. Even their system of mythology indeed clearly evinces, that a belief of this truth is congenial to the nature of man. Observations that tend to confirm these remarks shall precede, as usual, our account of the Platonic doctrine

on

on this subject, and of the arguments whereby it is supported.

It will occur to every man who has heard of polytheism, that its ceremonies and institutions are founded in the hope and belief of a future state, towards which they point with a precision that indicates their popular estimation. The plains of Elysium, the gloom of Tartarus, the bark of Cerberus, and the boat of Charon, the solitary margin of the Styx, and the oblivious water of Lethe, are indications of thought that carried its researches into regions wherein hope delights to expatiate. Poetry seized at an early period upon a tenet so pleasing to the powers of imagination, and went hand in hand with philosophy in describing the mansions and in pointing out the employments of the blessed *.

Of philosophers we may observe in general, that all who taught a metempsychosis, considered the soul as being distinct from matter, by the dissolution of which its existence cannot be affected. Thales taught that the spirit, proceeding originally from the Supreme Being, is re-united to him at the time of its separation from

* The classical reader need not here be referred to the Odyssey, and to the whole six books of the Æneid.

the

the body *. The Egyptian philosophers believed, according to Herodotus, that it came from heaven, and that it will return to this celestial mansion after having passed, during 2000 years, through various states of purification †. Anaxagoras, although he had no proper idea of the nature of the soul ‡, yet taught that it is immortal. Its incorporeal nature was one of the principles of the Aristotelian philosophy §. Finally, the opinion of the Pythagorean tribe of this subject is well known, as having corresponded with that of the philosophers above-mentioned ||. Although the members of the Italic school maintained this truth before life and immortality were brought to light, by arguments

---

* Cicero, ap. Lactan. lib. vi. c. 8.

† Herodot. Euterpe.

‡ Vid. Theod. de Græc. affect. Serm. v. p. 547, 548, as quoted by Boyle, Art. Anaxag. & Aug. de Civitat. Dei, v. i. lib. ii. p. 650.

§ Λεγει (Αριστοτελις;) την Ψυχην ειναι ασωματον, εντελιχειαν ουσαν την πρωτην· σωματος γαρ φυσικυ και οργανικυ δυναμει ζωην εχοντας. Laert. lib. v. p. 322. I have quoted the words of Laertius here, because Augustine seems to consider this philosopher's notion of the soul as being the same as that of Anaxagoras above-mentioned. Aristoteles *quintum* corpus eam dixit esse. Ibid. v. ii. lib. xxii. p. 700. His learned commentator refutes this assertion at great length. Est Aristoteles concretione omni compositionique ac corpore animum liberat, &c. p. 701. Vid. et Cicer. Oper. tom. iv. p. 355.

|| Diogen. Laert. Pythag.

of which the amount was probability, it is yet certain that some of its most eminent scholars found in the belief of immortality a source of solid and permanent felicity *.

Of poets we may observe, that Homer, who, it must be confessed, does not treat his deities

* I grant that Cicero is not at all times equally explicit in maintaining the Platonic doctrine of immortality, which Cæsar in his celebrated speech, recorded by Sallust, seems wholly to reprobate. V. Bell. Catalin. The language of the former, however, when he seems to doubt of this truth, is feeble, and betrays the fluctuation that arises from imperfect evidence. Etiam si non sit mihi tamen persuadere vitam. Si non ero, sensu omni caribo, &c. Epist. lib. vi. Ep. 3. But who will compare these and a few similar expressions, principally scattered through his Epistles, with his reasoning in defence of this doctrine in his admired treatise De Senectute, in that entitled Consolatio, or (not to mention other parts of his writings) with the beautiful description of his Somnium Scipionis? It is in these parts of his writings that we find the real sentiments of this great man disclosed without reserve on a subject that is to rational beings of all others the most important. His doubts and apparent hesitation, so feebly urged, and so readily retracted, exhibit, in one view, the most convincing evidence of the expedience, or rather of the necessity, of a revelation from God. The learned reader will find, upon examination, a striking resemblance between the observations of Cicero in his Cato Major, c. 21. and those of Socrates in a dialogue of Æschines, entitled Axiochus, in which the question is examined, whether death ought to be feared? Dial. iii. p. 166.

with

with much respect, yet adheres at all times to the doctrine of future retribution.

Αλλα σεις' Ηλυσιον πεδιον, και πειρατα γαιης
Αθανατοι πεμψυσι
τη περ ρηιστη βιοτη *.

Every classical reader knows, that in order to learn the sentiments of the great Roman poet on this subject, as corresponding with those of his predecessor, we must transcribe compleatly his sixth Eneid.

Among ancient writers who are advocates of immortality Plato is undoubtedly pre-eminent, not only as the various evidences of this truth are explained and illustrated in his other writings, but as one of his most laboured performances is wholly employed in establishing it upon the foundation of argument. Of his principal observations I shall here endeavour to exhibit a summary, as containing whatever unassisted reason cannot suggest with efficacy on the subject.

In order to demonstrate a truth, in the belief of which human misery has its surest refuge,

* Odys. Origen. cont. Cel. p. 350.

our author considers successively the following circumstances: 1. The nature of the soul, as a being distinct from matter, to which its operations are wholly dissimilar. 2. Its desires and infinite capacity, which are the surest evidences of its immortality. 3. Its moral perfection, if we may thus term it, which is constituted by its congeniality and resemblance to the Divine Mind, the source of perfection and of happiness. 4. Its present situation, its hope of advancement, and the unequal distribution of reward and punishment, 5. Its pre-existence, &c. on which we have already made some observations. 6. Our great philosopher refutes the objections to which his theory is exposed, and makes some remarks upon the nature of that state into which the soul will be admitted when emancipated from the present.

1. Whatever may be affirmed concerning the notions which other philosophers conceived of the nature of the human soul, its immateriality is a fundamental principle in the writings of Plato, from which his subsequent reasoning on this subject derives its efficacy. Thus, in different parts of his writings he applies to the mind the terms εμφρον, ασωματον, μανοειδον, as being expressive of that intelligence, spirituality, and simplicity, whereby it is peculiarly distinguished

guished from unintelligent, corporeal, and compounded substance *. Our author enlarges alternately with this purpose on the power which the mind exerts, on the objects which it contemplates, and on the offices which it is employed in discharging. Its power is exerted, as we have already seen, in controuling appetites, and subduing passions, which have their origin in its union with matter, whereby its operations are sometimes disturbed and interrupted. Its objects are sometimes of a mutable nature in consequence of this union, as being seen through the medium of sense; and are sometimes pure and eternal. While employed in the former contemplation, the mind wanders from one point to another, as the scenes vary that are presented to the senses, and being affected by the mutability of its objects, is like a man under the influence of intoxication. When on the contrary, retiring within itself, it dwells upon immutable subjects that are congenial to its nature, it unites itself with ease to whatever has permanent excellence, and the actions of a spirit thus uniformly regulated, are said to be directed by wisdom. The soul therefore that conceives ideas of what is pure, eternal, unchangeable, resembles the Divine Being, of whom alone those perfections are characteristical. It has, on the

* Epinom. Repub. lib. x. Phæd.

contrary,

contrary, no similarity to material substances, which are constantly fluctuating: its essence, simple and uncompounded, as is that of its original, cannot be dissolved, and is therefore immortal *.

Attentive at all times to the distinction between matter and spirit, Plato, in mentioning the offices in which the soul is occupied, observes, that this pure intelligence lays aside the body as much as possible in its search after abstracted truths, that have no connection with it. It ascends therefore at some times in its proper sphere to the great original of excellence, whose perfections it delights to contemplate, and whose nature it is solicitous to investigate †. While thus employed, the grosser appetites cease for a season to disturb its research. It lays aside as much as possible the pleasures, the appetites, the pains, the terrors, to which it is exposed in the intercourse of society ‡. But it finds the attempt to repel at all times corporeal influence to be impracticable upon experiment. Passions that precipitate the thought, and appetites that are clamorous for gratification, disturb

* Plat. Phed. Oxon. Typograph. Clarendin.
† Epinom.
‡ Φιλοσοφου Ψυχη απεχιται των ηδονων τι και επιθυμιων, και λυπων και φοβον καθ οσον δυναται. Ibid. p. 223.

the

the soul in her seat of pure contemplation, and overshade the serenity of her aspect. Hence Socrates concludes with great probability, that of two consequences one must necessarily follow; either that we can never discover truth, or that we must discover it after death, for then, and not sooner, will the soul be separated for ever from its incumbrance *. Upon this foundation, therefore, he builds his conclusion, that a true philosopher ought to look forward with confidence and satisfaction to that moment of separation which we denominate death, as the instant at which he will be emancipated from a prison, from which he languished to be released †.

2. To the immateriality of the soul, as affording a proof of its future existence, Plato adds observations which tend to confirm this doctrine on its desires and capacity. As the soul, after having explored inferior objects, finds its chief good in contemplating the divine nature and perfections which cannot be comprehended in its present state, the desire of immortality, which is implanted in every heart, has operated in all ages most powerfully upon the best and worthiest of mankind ‡. Our author considers, or rather follows this desire in its various effects,

* Ibid. p. 179.   † p. 182.
‡ Conviv. Platon. Oper. p. 1197.

according

according to the characters and dispositions of men: and after having followed, until he loses it in the contemplation of Supreme excellence, concludes, that he who by this contemplation, and by the practice of virtue, becomes the friend of God, will, (if any man can obtain it,) be finally rewarded with the eternal enjoyment of him *. Upon the whole, he considers that pure and refined love which renders meditation on the divine perfections a delightful exercise in this life, as an indication of that recompence which will be conferred upon it in another.

Our prospect of immortality is brightened, according to the Platonic doctrine, by the consideration of the vast capacity of the human soul. That spirit, says Socrates, which from building cities, and establishing commonwealths, ascends to the contemplation of the heavens, marks the revolutions of the celestial bodies, observes the courses of the sun and moon, calculates the eclipses of those bodies, and foretels their immediate restoration; considers the equinoctial phænomena, or double returns of the sun †;
brings

---

* Ibid. p. 1200.
† This constellation consisting of seven small stars in Taurus, which rise about the vernal equinox, were much attended to by the ancients, on account of the rain and stormy

brings intelligence from the pleiades concerning the seasons, winds, showers, storms, and whirlwinds; that spirit which comprehends so many great objects, cannot be annihilated at death. It will enjoy perfect happiness in an immortal state *, &c. Add to these remarks on the natural capacity of the soul, what Plato mentions concerning its contempt of inferior pursuits †, and aspiration after the knowledge and fruition of the Divine Mind, on which he represents it as being fed and invigorated ‡; and some view will be formed of the argument for immortality, that arises from the soul's capacity and comprehension.

3. Our observations on that moral perfection whereby this spirit is peculiarly assimilated to Deity, are, in a great measure, anticipated by former views of this subject. Our author's declarations on it occur so frequently, and are so explicit and particular, that an enumeration of these at much length is rendered unnecessary. The soul, as being a substance, wholly distinct

---

stormy weather that accompanied their appearance. Hence their name in Greek is derived from the word πλειν, to navigate, from the dangers to which sailors were exposed at the time of their appearance.

* Vid. Æschin. Axioch. ubi sup.
† Platon. Oper. p. 126.
‡ Repub. Lib. vi.

from

from the body of man, is, in the Platonic idea, eternal, and cannot have an end, because it never had a beginning*: it is allied to God as the consequence of participating his nature †: it acts in its proper sphere, when it aspires after the knowledge of that Being to whom it is conscious of bearing a resemblance ‡: a virtuous man is therefore the most perfect image of God in this world §; and at death the spirit which bears so many signatures of likeness to Deity ‖, will return to its original, and may look forward to that event in the contemplation of virtuous actions, with confidence and satisfaction **.

4. The most decisive arguments that can be urged in behalf of a future state, are those which will be suggested to a reflecting mind by the present situation of man, by his hope of immortality, and by an apparent inequality, and indeed injustice, in the immediate distribution of reward and punishment. The discerning mind of our great philosopher appears to have dwelt

---

* Platon. Phœd.

† Ομοιος ιϛι τω Θιω, και αθανατω, και νοητω, και μονοιδει, &c. Phœdon.

‡ Repub. Lib. vi.

§ Thætet. and Epinom.

‖ Αξυνθετος, αιδης, αδιαφθαρος, αθανατος.

** De Legib. Lib. xii.

successively on these evidences of immortality, which are explained and enforced in different parts of his writings.

Man, in the judgment of Plato, is, as we have already seen, an imperfect creature, exposed to natural and necessary evils, which he can neither foresee nor prevent. He is the inhabitant of a world, well indeed adapted to the gross and corrupted part of his nature; but ill suited to the faculties of a pure and divine intelligence. We appear to those who occupy superior regions, as ants and frogs do to us, scattered along the surface of an immense mass abounding in inequalities, enveloped in a gross atmosphere, darkened by clouds, and overflowed with water *. Of this mass, we have followed our author in examining the constituent parts, and in observing the formation. We have seen in what manner evil was introduced into it according to his principles, and we must now consider man as animated by the hope of being translated to a scene that is exempted from vicissitude. This delightful hope is at once the pledge of immortality, and the

* Και ημας οικεν τους μεχρις Ηρακλειων ςηλων απο φασιδος, εισ μικρω τινι μοριω ωσπερ περι τελμα μυρμηκας η βατραχης περι την θαλατταν οικουντας. Ειναι γαρ περι την γην πολλα κοιλα και παντοδαπα, &c. Phed. p. 290.

most powerful incentive to virtue*. It is the pledge of immortality, because it originates in a dissatisfaction with present enjoyments, and a solicitude about the objects of a future state, which indicates their existence †. It operates at the same time as a stimulus to the practice of every virtue, by rendering the toil supportable that leads to the enjoyment of the highest reward ‡.

Amidst arguments for immortality drawn from the nature, desires, and powers of the human mind; from its congeniality to the nature and aspiration to the enjoyment of God; from its present situation, and the hope whereby it is at all times animated and supported; Plato is not inattentive to the great moral evidence of this doctrine, the present imperfect and apparently unequal distribution of reward and punishment. Having established as a principle, that God is intimately acquainted with the characters of men, as they are distinguished by being just or unjust, he observes, that the former must be beloved, and the latter hated by him, without

---

* Τουτων δε ενικα χρη ων διεληλυθαμεν παντα ποιειν ωστε αρετης και φρονησεως εν τω βιω μετασχειν· Καλον γαρ το αθλον, και η ΕΛΠΙΣ ΜΕΓΑΛΗ. p. 304.

† Symp. Repub. Lib. x.

‡ Phedon. ubi sup.

regard to external circumstances or situation. Poverty therefore, he says, diseases, or whatever in this life we denominate *evil*, will conduce to the happiness of a virtuous man either here or hereafter: for he who by the study and exercise of virtue attempts to become assimilated to the Divine Mind, will finally obtain from him an adequate reward. This remark is enforced by illustrations, for which we must refer the reader to the original*. In the same spirit he enforces the proof of immortality from the justice of God, in another part of his writings, as being interested in the reward of virtuous, and in the punishment of bad actions, in the state after death †.

5. The arguments in behalf of a future state, as far as these have yet been examined, are such, as although few men perhaps would have discovered, yet all will comprehend, and approve. But the doctrine of pre-existence may be regarded particularly as a Platonic dogma, when we consider it in the present point of view ‡. To observations that have already been made on this tenet, originally of the Pythagorean school §,

---

* P. 759.
† Platon. Gorg. p. 523.
‡ P. 195. et ubi sup.
§ Cicer. Tusc. Quest. l. v. c. 3. Digen. Laert. in proem.

it is here only proper to add, that our author's notion of pre-existence is not founded, as those of his master, Pythagoras, are said to have been, upon distinct remembrance of certain events*. The sum of his argument, as it is detailed by Plutarch, is, that as the mind received existence before the creation of the body, we may reasonably conclude that it will survive its dissolution †.

2. In bringing forward, and establishing those direct proofs of immortality, which have been laid before the reader, Plato is particularly attentive to obviate objections to which he was aware that his theory lay open. Without mentioning incidental questions which arise from various points in the course of his dialogues, the friends of Socrates propose two difficulties in the dialogue entitled Phedon, which he employs some time in solving to their satisfaction. One is, that what we denominate the soul, is an harmony arising from an exact proportion of the various members of the body corresponding to each other, and that it is more or less perfect, according to the aptitude of these proportions. In this sense it is fitly compared to the music of an harp, whose strings are perfectly modu-

* Plut. de Anim. Procreat. Op. v. ii. p. 1016.
† Phed. p. 230, &c.

lated to each other; and the instrument thus tuned, is the body from which it proceeds. The qualities, say the objectors, of immateriality, indivisibility, &c. may all be predicated of this harmony, or musical concord, as much as of what we term the soul: and we might affirm with equal propriety, that the harmony remains, or ought to remain, after we have broken the instrument, as that the spirit subsists after the dissolution of the body. The second objection proceeds upon the supposition, that the mind, although it be a substance distinct from body, and superior to it, is not therefore indissoluble. It is urged, that after having animated perhaps many corporeal frames, it decays gradually, and expires in the last body, as a man dies after having worn different suits of clothes.

In answering the former objection, Socrates is not satisfied to prove, that the idea of an harmony arising from corporeal proportions, and constituting the governing principle, is incompatible with the former doctrine of pre-existence, which his hearers had concurred in acknowledging to be well founded. He enters more closely into the subject; and while he adheres to the strict meaning of the term harmony, or concord, demonstrates by the following arguments the futility of this hypothesis.

He

He observes in the first place, that harmony depends upon the perfection of the instrument, and is injured by any accident whereby it may be disordered. But it is surely otherwise with the soul of man, which is independent of the body, and is at all times opposed to it. Of concordant sounds we observe in the same manner, that the harmony is more or less perfect, according to the temperament or constitution of the parts from which it arises; and we apply to it those epithets with propriety, as it approaches towards or recedes from a certain standard. But these terms cannot be applied to the soul, as being rendered by any operation whatever more or less spiritual, if we may thus express it, without the greatest absurdity. Again, when we speak of virtue and vice, the former as constituting harmony, and the latter discord in life, we must consider that which is incongruous and dissonant, if the soul be essentially a concord, as proceeding from a source or principle of which incongruity is destructive. As harmony therefore, properly so called, admits not of discordant vibrations, so neither would the soul, considered as a concord, admit of vicious propensities. Lastly, in music the harmony arises from the instrument, but in man, the soul commands the body, which it can at all times retain in subjection. It repels its appetites, contra-
dicts

dicts its desires, moderates its passions, cures its diseases, governs it with an authority which it cannot resist, and imposes upon it pennance, to which it submits with reluctance. In no sense whatever, therefore, can the mind, or intelligent principle in man, be defined an harmony, which originates in corporeal symmetry or proportion.

Socrates having obviated in this manner the first objection respecting the nature of the soul, proceeds to remove the second, which regards its duration. Here the philosopher has recourse to one of the most ingenious theories of his Phedon, that principles diametrically opposite cannot meet and subsist together in the same subject, any more than the constituent forms of odd and even in the same number *. The soul therefore, which is the principle of animation in all bodies whatever, and is properly denominated *life*, cannot admit death, that is opposite to, and would be destructive of it, into its bosom; according to a rule of unalterable permanency, which he explains at great length, and enforces by particular examples †.

* P. 191, &c.
† P. 282.

3. The third great point to which our attention is called in examining the Platonic doctrine on the subject of immortality, relates to the employments and state of those spirits which are released from the cares and vicissitudes of life.

One of the most conclusive arguments in behalf of future existence, arises from that restless curiosity whereby the mind of man is impelled, in its present state, to pry into subjects which it is forbidden to investigate, and to contemplate regions of which it cannot discover the boundary, or be made known to the inhabitants. To this passionate desire, so ardent in the pursuit of this species of information, we must ascribe the conjectures which men have indulged in all ages concerning the exercises of the unbodied spirit, and its mode of enjoyment and occupation. He who would examine the writings of the ancients on these matters with attention and accuracy, after having selected the points wherein all are agreed, ought carefully to distinguish the reveries of imagination in a field on which it delights to expatiate, from tenets that are consonant to reason and to philosophy.

When we consider the present subject with this object in view, we shall find, that the wisdom of of antiquity adopts as irrefragable one great maxim; that the soul of man was originally a portion of the Divine Mind, to whom, if it be not polluted by its union with matter in this inferior situation, it returns at the moment of dissolution. "Let us hasten (says one of the followers of Zoroaster,) to be reunited to the light of the great Father of Nature, from whom the human soul containing many inferior intelligences, originally came *" Again—The soul participates of the nature of God. It contains nothing mortal, but is wholly assimilated to the Divinity †. Epicharmus in the same manner maintained, that man is compounded of two parts, body and spirit, of which each goes back at death to the place from which it sprung, the body to dust, and the soul to the celestial region ‡. It is true indeed, that, according to the Pythagorean philosophy, many purifications were necessary, in order to render the spirit that had been contaminated in its earthly mansion, fitted for the participation of divine enjoy-

---

* Χρη τε σπευδειν προς το Φαος, και προς πατρος Αυγας;
  Ενθεν επεμφθη σοι Ψυχη πολυν εσσαμενη Νουν.

† Ψυχη η μεροπων θεον αγξει πως εις εαυτον
  Ουδεν θνητον εχουσα ολη θεοθεν μεμετρυται.

  Sybill. Orac. v. ii. p. 79.

‡ Plut. De Consol. Op. v. ii. p. 110

ment,

ment *. But the souls of virtuous men were placed, as soon as they left the body, in a state of happiness suited to their nature and original. Plutarch, (who quotes with approbation the opinion of Epicharmus;) considers man in his present situation as in exile †. At death, he tells us, that the spirit which had been polluted by the practice of vice, suffers the punishment that is due to it: but those, on the contrary, whose actions have rendered them acceptable to God, after having been purified from the remains of corruption in an unpolluted region, return into their native land with ineffable delight, as men who are recalled from banishment, into the country that is the object of their desires ‡. Apollonius, the impostor of Tyana, comforts his fellow-prisoners, the captives of Domitian, by a similar consideration. The period, says he, which we denominate life, is passed by the pure and intelligent spirit in a state of improvement, wherein it bears with reluctance the evils of humanity §. Aristotle, whose declarations on this subject are not always explicit ||, appears in his account of Eudamas, as quoted by Cicero,

---

* Herod. Lib. ii. Diogen. Laert. Art. Pythag.
† Plutarch. v. ii. p. 943.
‡ Id. ibid. p. 607.
§ Philostrat. Vit. Apollon. p. 468.
|| Cicer. Tusc. Quest. l. i. Op. v. iv. p. 355.

to have adopted sentiments that coincide in every circumstance with those of the authors already mentioned *. The illustrious Roman philosopher and orator maintains, as we have already seen, the same principles as the former in all parts of his writings. " The spirit, he says, that feels, that reflects, that lives, that reasons; which remembers the past, comprehends the present, provides for the future; to which, among the objects around us, we perceive nothing that bears similarity; had a celestial and divine original. It came from God, whom alone it resembles, as being pure and uncontaminated †. It is in its present state imprisoned, unhappy, restless, the sport of calamities, which press upon it on all sides: the hour of death is that of liberaration, when it shakes off the shackles that invest it, *returns* into its native regions, and blesses the moment at which the key of the last messenger opened to it the gate of immortality ‡."

From these and many similar observations, which open upon all sides in the writings of the ancients, we may judge of opinions which philosophers conceived of the nature of the soul, as being allied to the Divinity in its present state,

* Id. De Divin. lib. i. Oper. p. 446.
† De Divin. Oper. p. 359 and 475.
‡ Id. De Divin. p. 446, and Confol.

and of its employment in those abodes to which it flies, or rather into which it returns at the hour of separation.

It will no doubt occur to the intelligent reader, that in this enumeration no mention is made of the sensual pleasures, or of punishments that correspond to those which we inflict: the stone of Sisiphus, the water of Tantalus, the vulture of Prometheus, or the wheel of Ixion. These fabulous and fanciful representations, the embellishments of poetry and admiration of the vulgar, were rejected by reason in her hour of calm contemplation, for objects more suitable to the subject. Of real philosophers we may observe, that when they represent the happiness of a future state, by scenes and exercises which are at present the most familiar and agreeable, they have most commonly one of two purposes in view. This is either that of influencing the actions of men in general, and particularly of young persons, by motives adapted to excite attention, or that of accommodating their discourse most efficaciously to the circumstances of individuals, on the loss of friends, or in the prospect of dissolution, by bringing before them pleasing objects which soothe and captivate imagination. It is thus that Plutarch consoles Apollonius on the death of his son [*]; Cicero

[*] Plut. Consol. Oper. v. ii. p. 121.

alleviates

alleviates by anticipation the infirmities of age *; and Socrates fortifies Axiochus against the terrors of approaching death †. They considered the axiom, that happiness or misery in a future state will be consequent on the conduct of the present, as being established both by reason and philosophy; and they selected amidst various motives or arguments, those that were fitted with greatest propriety to the circumstances or situation of the person whom they addressed.

These observations, while they give some general idea of the doctrine and opinions of the ancients, may throw some light on that of Plato, which I now proceed to examine.

He who studies attentively the philosophy of this author will find, that he mentions three states distinct from each other, as being prepared for the departed spirit. Of those, the first and principal is the mansion of the Gods in the celestial regions, with whom the souls of the just enjoy perfect felicity; the second, or middle state, is that of ΑΔΗΣ or ΑΔΕΙΑΣ, from the term signifying sad or dark, as being properly applied to its purpose, and to the exercises of its inhabitants; the last, is that of Tartarus, pro-

* De Senectut.
† Æschin. ubi sup.

perly

perly so called, a gulph into which the finally impenitent were plunged without hope of release.

1. Of the states thus enumerated Socrates modestly expresses his hope, in the dialogue entitled Phedon, of being admitted into the assembly of good men, and into that particularly where the Gods diffuse uninterrupted felicity. In order to render his discourse on this subject entertaining as well as instructive to young men, who were attracted most naturally by sensible representations, he enters into a sublime description of the superior regions of heaven, the habitation of the Gods, and of the spirits of the just. From a land blessed with a perpetual temperature of season,

> Where from the breezy deep the bless'd inhale
> The fragrant murmurs of the western gale [*],

from sacred groves and temples inhabited by the Gods, who are the companions of those to whom they utter their oracles; from happy isles enveloped in pure circumfluent æther, these happy beings cast an eye of pity upon us, scattered, as we have already seen, on the banks of rivers, or along the shores of the ocean, as ants or frogs, who have scooped out holes for their residence in

---

[*] Phed. p. 292, &c.

the neighbourhood of a marsh, or of some other place, provided with air and water. And it is, he says, on account of the gross and fœtid air which we breath in this impure region, which is only the sediment of the other, that we cannot see what is transacting in it, and in the habitation of the blessed.

From this paradisiacal scene, our author represents those whose minds are enlightened by knowledge, and purified by contemplation, as being translated to more refined and perfect enjoyment, suited to the pure spirit disencumbered of body; the nature of which it is not easy to describe, or comprehend.

2. It is not my present business to examine the various significations of the term ΑΔΗΣ, by which Origen and the primitive Christians in general certainly meant the mansion of the dead, or receptacle of souls when separated from the body *. It is used here as a term expressive of
that

* The opinion of Origen on this subject is obvious, from a passage already quoted in his remark on the story of Er, the Armenian, as mentioned by Plato. Of this man he says, απηγγελκεναι τα περι των εν ΑΔΟΥ. ubi sup. Hades is here obviously the receptacle of departed souls, into which, according to many of the fathers, and not into hell, in the more modern acceptation of that word, the soul of our
Saviour

that state, wherein spirits which had been polluted by their residence in corporeal forms, were purified and fitted, in the judgment of Plato, for entering into the mansions of the blessed.

Of the means whereby this purification is accomplished, it is not of much importance to inquire. The terms ευα and εκπυρωσις, used by Platonists and Stoics with the same purpose, seem to point at a purification effected by fire in a separate state, somewhat similar to the doctrine of the Church of Rome on this subject. It is of more consequence to know, that our author considers the souls of men in their situation in three different points of view. Those whose minds were enlightened by the knowledge of philosophy, and whose lives were uniformly regulated by the practice of virtue, ascended at death first, as we have already seen, to a purer and happier region than the present, and at last into the mansion of the Gods. The second class consists of persons, who having been guilty of great, although not of inexpiable crimes, are consigned to punishments, which although severe, are yet permitted to terminate as soon as their purpose is accomplished The

---

Saviour migrated after his death, and remained to the day of his resurrection. Hence the article in the Creed, He descended into HELL. The third he arose, &c.

last order is of those whose guilt being of such magnitude as cannot be pardoned, are given up to torments of unceasing duration.

In order to render his doctrine on this subject adapted to general comprehension, Socrates speaks of an immense abyss, into which four mighty rivers roll their tides: the gulph into which they descend is named Tartarus. Hither criminals of every denomination are at first precipitated, after having taken their trial. Those whose bad actions are expiated by suffering, are thrown up by the river, and at last released from their misery. Unceasing punishment is inflicted only on the perpetrators of aggravated and accumulated crimes, who are no longer objects of divine forgiveness *.

I observe only farther on this subject, that the Pythagorean and Platonic metempsychosis is undoubtedly a state of purification wherein the soul was gradually prepared for reascending to its native regions, by passing through different states, and being engaged in occupations whereby this purpose was gradually accomplished. It has, I know, been urged with some apparent reason, that this doctrine of metempsychosis is

* P. 302.

inconsistent with that which we have been attempting to explain, concerning future reward and punishment. But it ought to be observed, that our author mentions the rewards conferred on a life of uniform virtue, or the punishments inflicted on crimes of enormous magnitude, or the expiation necessary for those of a very particular nature, as offering violence to a parent, killing a man in passion, &c. in the preceding account *. In ordinary cases, the third purgation as it was denominated, or state through which the mind passed without being contaminated, was reckoned sufficient to qualify it for entering into the mansions of the blessed †.

Our great philosopher having thus examined the nature, and evinced the immortality of the soul, makes the proper use of his observations

* Id. ibid.

† The classical reader will be pleased to see this tenet in the language of Pindar:

Οσοι δ'ετολμησαν ις τρις
Εκατεραθι μεινοντες,
Απο παμπαν αδικων εχειν
Ψυχαν, ετειλαν Διος
Οδον παρα χρονε τυρσιν·
Ε.θα Μακαρων
Νασον ωκεανιδες
Αυραι περιπνευσιν, &c.

Olymp. 2d.

on this subject, by exhorting his disciples to consider the care of this divine intelligence, as being, in the language of inspired writers, the one thing needful. "If, says he, the soul be immortal, your attention ought to be employed in improving and in watching over it, as being framed to live not only during the present, but in all time whatever. It is, therefore, highly dangerous to neglect its interest. If death, indeed, were the dissolution of the whole man, the bad part of the species would be unexpectedly fortunate, in being exempted at the time when they leave the world, from the punishment of crimes which they committed in it, and in being liberated in this manner, at the same instant, from their souls, their bodies, and their vices. But now, when we have evinced that the soul is immortal, no subterfuge nor safety remains to bad men, unless in purifying it for its new state by every salutary means; for the spirit carries nothing along with it in its separate state, but the principles and instructions that have been impressed upon it, which begin to operate either to its advantage or prejudice, at the instant of its arrival *."

Thus

---

* Ει μιν γαρ η ο θανατος του παντος απαλλαγη, ερμαιον αν ην τοις κακοις αποθνησι, του τε σωματος αμα απηλλαχθαι, και της αυτων κακιας μετα της Ψυχης. Νυν δε επειδη αθανατος φαινεται ουσα, ουδεμια αν

Thus I have laid before the reader a summary of the arguments by which Plato became himself convinced of a truth, and impressed the belief of it upon the minds of his disciples, without the knowledge of which man might envy the condition of the reptile upon which he treads. "Let no useless parade, says he, in the full conviction of immortality, be made about the dead. The body, which follows the soul while the man lives, presents only the lifeless image of him when he is gone. The immortal spirit goes to the Gods, to render an account of its actions; an account, to which good men will look forward with confidence; but a cause of terror to the bad, who, after death, can have no advocate. To the dead we cannot be of use. Our business is, to give every instructive lesson to the living, that they may be prevented, by persevering in virtuous practice in this life, from suffering under the punishment of final impenitence in that which is to come *."

It

ειη αυτη αλλη αποφυγη κακων, ηδε σωτηρια, πλην ω; βελτιστη τε και φρονιμωτατην γινεσθαι· Ουδεν γαρ αλλο τις ΑΔΟΥ η Ψυχη ερχεται, πλην της παιδειας και τη τροφης· Α δη και λεγεται μεγιστα ωφελειν η βλαπτειν τον τελευτησαντα ευθυς εν αρχη της εκεισε πορειας. Phedon. p. 286, &c.

* De Legib. Lib. xii. He who chooses to consult the Phedon of Plato, will find in it many ingenious arguments, and beautiful illustrations, which are not mentioned here.

It will occur to any attentive reader from a review of the preceding observations on this subject, that strenuous advocates of immortality arise on all sides among ancient philosophers. But was it by philosophers only that this doctrine was taught? or did it originate in polished and cultivated ages?—Let us contemplate in imagination the first objects which history offers to the examination of mankind. Let us ascend to the founders; let us penetrate the recesses of the mausoleums of Egypt. We shall find that these were constructed as the receptacles of bodies, near which the spirit was believed to reside, and which, in the revolution of ages, it was destined to reanimate *.

If, from these magnificent monuments of human conviction, we turn our eyes towards nations in the first and simplest periods of manners and society, the belief of this great truth, as characterising mankind in general, will strike an intelligent reader, in their festivals, ceremonies, deifications, and ritual observances, of which it is here unnecessary to enumerate ex-

---

The author has endeavoured to select those arguments, which, while they appear to be conclusive, are best adapted to general comprehension.

* Herodot. ubi sup. Also Univ. Hist. vol. i. p. and Savary's Lettr. sur L'Egypt. Lett. xxvi.

amples.

amples. From the altars of Greece in her earliest stage of progression, to the Pagodas of India; from the mausoleum of Artemisia*, to the Morai of Oberea †, the same persuasion of future existence appears to be an essential article in the creed of mankind; who in opposite regions of the globe, practising different rites, and regulated by contrary customs, are yet animated by *one hope* in the journey of life, and look forward with one consent to the regions of immortality.

Among philosophers in more enlightened ages it will be acknowledged, that Plato takes the lead from all who were unacquainted with revelation, in maintaining the truth of this doctrine, and in establishing it firmly upon the basis of argument. He seems, indeed, to have exhausted the subject in different parts of his writings, wherein he has alternately advanced in examining it, whatever human understanding could suggest of reason, or human ingenuity supply, of illustration. Hence most probably it has happened, that of his successors no indi-

---

* A pyramidical structure raised to the memory of her husband, by one of the most illustrious heroines of antiquity.

† Hawkesworth's Voyag. v. ii. and Lett. sur L'Egypt ubi sup.

vidual,

vidual, *directed merely by the light of nature*, has struck into a new path on the same field, or confirmed this doctrine by closer investigation. The great Roman philosopher, in particular, acknowledges in terms of admiration, the merit of his great original, to whose judgment he subscribes with confidence, and whose hope he embraces with exultation.

Let us remember, that in the prospect of immortality, established by proof, of which a summary has been presented to the reader, the most illustrious names that are recorded in history, were supported in the trials which preceded dissolution, and were animated at the moment when it approached. It was by these that Socrates was induced to make a libation from the draught that was to terminate his present existence, with the wish of being carried successfully on his journey. By this consolation he was supported in his last moments, when he told his friends, at the time when death was already in possession of the extreme parts of his body, that he was now about to *depart* or *retire* from them. At the distance of many ages, we behold the Roman patriot, the martyr of liberty,

* Ειπεν, οτι επιδαν προς τη καρδια γεννηται αυτο, τοτε οιχησεται. Phedon. a fin.

stretched

stretched on his bed, and in the transport which *those* evidences of immortality kindled in his heart; feeling about his pillow for the sword that was to emancipate the impatient spirit from its prison, into the regions of freedom and felicity. Finally, the proofs of future existence, which have been brought forward, were those, where the comprehensive mind of Cicero found consolation amidst the vicissitudes of an eventful life. In the bower of retirement—in the languor of exile—in the vale of age—amidst the horrors of proscription—in flight—in terror—in apprehension of imminent danger—and at the approach of death—the soul of this *last of Romans*, fortified by the principles, and animated by the spirit of the theology of Plato, went onward upon the whole with equanimity. To the impression of *these principles*, and of *those evidences of future existence*, we must ascribe that calm fortitude with which a mind, naturally timid, contemplated its exit, and his dignified invitation to the minion of Antony, while he stretched out his neck to the suspended weapon, " to approach and perform his office."

Ye votaries of pleasure, who, without examination or remorse, have heedlessly espoused the cause of infidelity! Ye leaders of the young and the unwary, who boast of the numbers who pronounce

nounce your names with acclamation; who, recoiling from the eye of that Being whom ye would have blotted out from the universe, would plunge, in the paroxysm of terrified apprehension, into the gulph of annihilation! Can ye hear the united voice of your species, claiming immortality as their birth-right, and exulting in the hope of possessing it, without being impressed by a conviction which ye cannot repel? Does not this truth flash upon your minds from every region, while you are employed in perusing the history of mankind? Does it not inform among the sages of antiquity every eye that is turned upon you with indignant reproach? Shall it be said, that the wisdom which formerly enlightened all nations is now concentrated within the contracted focus of a few Utopian philosophers, whom she has commissioned to loosen the bonds of society, to proclaim liberty to the captive, to enlarge the dominion of vice, and to encourage the practice of suicide, by announcing to their fellow men, that life and existence will terminate at the same instant? Alas! Methinks I hear in every corner the children of adversity, as well as the victims of age and decrepitude, complaining, that you have extinguished in their disconsolate hearts the last feeble ray that seemed to tremble beyond the grave upon the temple of happiness! But this purpose

pose ye can at best but partially effect. Ye will still behold, upon casting your eyes abroad, the delightful hope of immortality softening the couch of pain, and chearing the heart of labour; penetrating the homely cot, and animating the dejected spirit; darting, in short, through all space, and irradiating every part of the universe, unless, perhaps, the darkness of your own forlorn and solitary bosoms.

THE END.

This Day is published, in Two Vols.
Price 10s. Boards,

THE HISTORY OF THE POOR;

THEIR RIGHTS, DUTIES, AND THE LAWS RESPECTING THEM.

IN A SERIES OF LETTERS.

By THO. RUGGLES, Esq. F.A.S.

ONE OF HIS MAJESTY'S JUSTICES OF THE PEACE FOR THE COUNTIES OF ESSEX AND SUFFOLK.

ALSO,
In Two Pocket Volumes, (Price 6s. sewed)

THE BARRISTER;

OR,

STRICTURES

ON THE EDUCATION PROPER FOR THE BAR.

AND,
(Price 2s. 6d. sewed)

ORIGINAL POEMS,

ON

VARIOUS OCCASIONS.

By a LADY.
Revised by W. COWPER, Esq.
OF THE INNER TEMPLE.

ERRATA.

Page	Line	
5	4	*For* Oromages *read* Oromazes, *pass*:
8		Note, *for* Fixis *read* Ficin
10	19	*Dele* of
11	3	*read* framed
14	10	*For* kind *read* mind
15	7	*For* neither *read* either
17	11	*read* Timæus
18	7	*For* inordinate *read* subordinate
20	18	*read* φυσιως
24	17	*read* desideratum
47	10	*read* Θιου Δημιουργου
48	10	*of Note, read* errour
50	8	*For* conformed *read* deformed
54	3	*of Note, for* is *read* as
74	18	*read* oracular
75	12	*read* this
76	17	*read* συναρχοντες
88	4	*of Note, read* has
90	15	*For* concern *read* confirm
106	23	*For* senses *read* scenes
111	9	*For* Zedydan *read* Yezdan
117	1	*of Note, read* αποροπαιου
123	23	*Dele* to
147	23	*For* right *read* eight
148	22	*For* him *read* them
169		Note, *for* six books *read* sixth book.

www.ingramcontent.com/pod-product-compliance
Lightning Source LLC
Chambersburg PA
CBHW021815230426
43669CB00008B/758